RIGHT HONOURABLE INSULTS

By the same author:

Westminster Words (with Stephen Parker)
Honourable Insults
Parliamentary Sauce

RIGHT HONOURABLE INSULTS

A Stirring Collection of Insults and Invective

Compiled by the Rt Hon Greg Knight

Robson Books

Special edition for PAST TIMES

RIGHT HONOURABLE INSULTS
text © Greg Knight

9 8 7 6 5 4 3 2 1 0

PAST TIMES®

In memory of

the late Conservative MP
Sir David Lightbown

and the late Labour MP
Bob Cryer

two friends,
who in different ways were both dedicated
and worthy parliamentarians.

I miss them both.

CONTENTS

ACKNOWLEDGEMENTS

The author wishes to thank the following for their help, advice, suggestions and assistance: Nicholas Bennett, the late Dr John Blackburn MP, Simon Burns MP, Sir Sydney Chapman MP, Sebastian Coe, the late Bob Cryer MP, Rt Hon David Davis MP, Andrew Mitchell, the late Sir Nicholas Fairbairn QC MP, Rt Hon Sir Jeremy Hanley, Timothy Kirkhope Esq. MEP, the late Sir David Lightbown MP, Rt Hon Andrew Mackay MP, Rt Hon David Mellor QC, Patrick McLoughlin MP, Rt Hon The Lord Ryder, the late Sir John Stradling-Thomas MP, Arthur Worsley, Janet Knight and for her help generally, Teresa Sothcott.

The following books contain some excellent political stories, a few of which are recalled here and are acknowledged with grateful thanks:

An American Life by Ronald Reagan, published by Hutchinson, *The View from Number 11* by Nigel Lawson, published by Bantam Press, *The Making of a Prime Minister* by Harold Wilson, published by Weidenfeld & Nicholson, *Upwardly Mobile* by Norman Tebbit, published by Weidenfeld & Nicholson.

INTRODUCTION

Anyone who has paid the slightest attention to politics over the years will know that one of the main activities of our elected representatives is insulting each other. Even during a constructive debate, a politician will often take time out to be abusive to his or her opponent and sometimes to a colleague too.

Bile, insult, impudence and insolence are all part of a good debater's armoury. The crescendo of emotion, the torrent of abuse and the flash of bad temper are the ingredients which make a good political speech *great*. Anyone who has heard Denis (now Lord) Healey on his feet will realize how effective the use of ridicule during a speech can be. And anyone who has been captivated by an oration of Lord Hailsham will know that the occasional use of emotion and bile can be both compelling and devastating. It certainly ensures that the attention of the audience is firmly held by the speaker, which is a necessary prerequisite of a great speech. Thus, politicians sometimes use gratuitous abuse to enliven what they know is a dull brief. They are aware that the barb helps them to hold the floor and thereby get their message across.

There is also another explanation for the frequency of the political insult. In the chamber of either House the 'audience' is not an impartial gathering, waiting to be convinced by rational argument and reasoned discussion. Unlike a jury in court, those listening *are* partial and do have a vested interest in the outcome of the debate, regardless of the strength of argument for either side. In the present House of Commons, all MPs except one belong to a political party. Therefore, when a government minister is forced to defend some policy or initiative, generally Labour MPs will support him, even if William Hague and his team have adduced compelling arguments why the policy is wrong or even why the minister should be sacked. In this scenario, where the outcome depends on party whipping and not on the facts placed before the House, no wonder one of the weapons frequently deployed by all sides is the parliamentary insult.

This is not a twentieth-century phenomenon. Politicians have been spewing vitriol at each other through the centuries and, as we approach the millennium, the trend, although somewhat diminished, still shows no signs of abating. It has certainly ebbed somewhat, however, from the heady days of Gladstone and Disraeli and of Winston Churchill and F. E. Smith. The reason for this is undoubtedly the advent of the televising of parliamentary proceedings. Whatever else they do, politicians always have an eye on the electorate. They have to. And it did not take our MPs long to realize that the public do not like to see arm-waving, ranting and gratuitous abuse emanating from the TV set in their own front room.

These days therefore party leaders are more circumspect than their forebears. They have learned from President Ronald Reagan, the most effective political communicator the world has seen, that a message conveyed with a reassuring smile and some gentle self-deprecation can be devastatingly effective – and also popular with the voters. Being acerbic on television *can* work but there is a real danger that the lasting impression left with the viewer will not be one of the ridiculed victim but a negative image of the perpetrator, who appears as someone who is a rather mean and unpleasant sourpuss. So today's elected representatives are more careful about what they say in public and how they say it. They behave in a more responsible manner and as a consequence they are frequently dull and boring.

But not always! Detailed between the covers of this book are those occasions when politicians have thrown caution to the wind and sparks have flown. The book covers the best political caustic gems uttered on both sides of the Atlantic over the past one hundred years, right up to the present day.

As you will observe, the one class of person who is usually safe from the vitriol of an MP is the constituent. I emphasize *constituent*, rather than the general public, because it is the possession by a person of the power to vote for or against the MP, which makes all the difference. Votes do matter to our elected representatives and they know that a sharp rebuke or apparently unsympathetic ear can cost them electoral support. However, even the most forbearing Member can occasionally lose his composure when faced with a stubborn, silly or psychopathic elector. Once, in 1986, after it had taken me five and a half hours to travel the expected two-hour journey from London to my constituency, I arrived just ten minutes late for my advice bureau and was confronted with a ranting pensioner who expressed her outrage at having been kept waiting. I explained the reason for my slightly late appearance, adding that most doctors kept their patients waiting far longer than this without reproach and said I was sorry. For some reason this only made her worse – her arms began flailing and she started to become abusive. After my horrendous journey, I decided that I had had quite enough so I ordered her to leave and said that I was not prepared to give advice to someone so unreasonable, irrational and abusive. She left shouting darkly that she would never vote for me again. Deciding later that perhaps I had been a little harsh, I pondered whether I should send her a mollifying letter, so I asked my receptionist if she had taken down the old lady's address. She had. I glanced at her note and to her great surprise I started laughing. I realized that the old dear was not a constituent of mine at all and so couldn't possibly vote for me anyway: I had just vented my spleen on a constituent of my parliamentary neighbour Margaret Beckett and the old dear should not have attended my surgery in the first place! Some MPs are not so lucky, as you will find out later on.

Occasionally, parliamentary anger is vented in response to an abusive letter the MP has received. One response, that has been used from time to time by MPs of all parties, is the reply: 'Dear Sir, Today I received an abusive and insulting letter from some crackpot who has signed your name. I thought you should know at once about this outrage.'

Once I used a slightly different tack to reply to a letter I had been sent, again from a non-constituent, and which contained abusive and profane language. I wrote: 'Dear Sir, My secretary, being a lady, cannot type what I think of you. I, being an honourable man, cannot write it, but you, being neither, will understand what I mean.'

Even this is mild compared to what used to be written. Anthony Henry, who was an MP at the beginning of the eighteenth century, was once asked by a group of his constituents to vote against the Budget of 1714. Angered that they should have the temerity to write to try to influence his voting intentions, he replied: 'Gentlemen, I have received your letter about the excise, and I am surprised at your insolence at writing to me at all. You know, and I know, that I bought this constituency. You know, and I know, that I am now determined to sell it, and you know, what you think I don't know, that you are now looking out for another buyer, and I know, what you certainly don't know, that I have now found another constituency to buy.' As Henry's letter continued, he became more abusive, adding for good measure: 'About what you said about the excise, may God's curse light upon you all, and may it make your homes as open and as free to the excise officers as your wives and daughters have always been to me while I have represented your rascally constituency.'

The advent of universal suffrage, party selection committees and tabloid newspapers have regrettably destroyed such vitriol in constituency correspondence. Over the years MPs have moderated their response to criticisms from constituents and others, although many still get rightly annoyed when a voter writes to *demand* that the MP vote in a particular way.

It was Edmund Burke who, in 1974, neatly summed up the duties of our elected representatives, after some of his own constituents had demanded that he vote for a particular cause. While addressing his electors in Bristol he argued: 'A constituent's wishes ought to have great weight with their MP. It is his duty to prefer their interests to his own. But his unbiased opinion, his mature judgement, his enlightened conscience, he ought not to sacrifice to you. Your representative owes you, not his industry only, but his judgement; and he betrays, instead of serves you, if he sacrifices it to your opinion . . . government and legislation are matters of reason and judgement, and not of inclination.' Such is the proliferation of lobbyists and special interest groups today that Burke's 'law' should be printed on the back of every polling card to remind the public that our MPs are representatives and not delegates.

Finally, I would like to thank Members of both Houses of Parliament for their continuing vituperation towards each other, without which the compilation of this book would not have been possible.

Rt Hon Greg Knight
London
England

BLASTS
FROM THE
PAST

Lord North was probably the worst Prime Minister of all time, although, if his own resignation speech is anything to go by, Norman Lamont, the Chancellor sacked by John Major, would probably dispute this. Certainly North's foreign policy was disastrous. He was, however, a witty speaker who was generally good-natured in debate.

One of his constant critics was an MP called Temple Luttrell. When Luttrell sarcastically remarked that he hoped his contribution to the debate would not 'clog the activity of government', North silenced him with the riposte: 'No more than a fly which, landing on the wheels of a chariot, thinks that it has raised the dust with which it is surrounded.'

The Duke of Wellington was one of the rudest men of his day. He was Prime Minister for nearly three years from January 1828 to November 1830, returning for a mere three weeks in 1834.

He always spoke his mind and certainly did not suffer fools at all: two traits that would certainly bar him from office today. He was completely out of touch with the electorate and had no knowledge whatsoever of trade or commerce. He admitted he did not know how to flatter and when this was put to him by a colleague who praised Sir Robert Peel, he retorted: 'I may have no small talk but Robert Peel has no manners.'

When, at a reception, two French marshals, still smarting over their battlefield defeat, turned their backs on him, he remarked loudly: 'It doesn't bother me, I have seen their backs before!'

He was, however, even-handed in dispensing insults, frequently insulting his own troops. Of the British cavalry then, he said: 'The only thing that they can be relied on to do is to gallop too far and too fast.'

He later opined: 'There is nothing on earth so stupid as a gallant officer.'

Diarist Doctor Samuel Johnson took a keen interest in the politics of his day. When a colleague boasted of his patriotism, Johnson uttered perhaps his most famous retort: 'Patriotism is the last refuge of a scoundrel.'

He had a low opinion of Tory Prime Minister Lord North, of whom he dismissively said: 'He fills a chair.'

On newcomers he opined: 'We are inclined to believe those whom we do not know because they have never deceived us.'

He had no time for the sport of angling, which led to the utterance of perhaps his second most famous retort. He defined the practice as: 'A stick and a piece of string with a worm on one end and a fool at the other.'

He accurately summed up his fellow countrymen: 'When two Englishmen meet, their first talk is of the weather.'

Edmund Burke, speaking of his opponents: 'They defend their errors as if they were defending their inheritance.'

On our revenue collection system: 'To tax and to please, no more than to love and be wise, is not given to men.'

On being in government: 'Those who have been once intoxicated with power, and have derived any kind of emolument from it, even though but for one year, can never willingly abandon it.'

And his view of politicians: 'I am convinced that we have a degree of delight in the real misfortunes of others.'

Clever he certainly was, but those with the most brains are not always the most interesting or stimulating orators. Burke was so dull and boring when addressing the Commons that he earned the nickname 'The Dinner Bell'. As soon as he rose to his feet, the majority of MPs decided it was time to take some refreshment in the Members' Dining Room.

Lord Macaulay, formerly Thomas Babington Macaulay, frequently enlivened nineteenth-century debate in the House of Lords. He once snapped at a colleague: 'It is possible to be below flattery as well as above it.'
•
Commenting about Socrates he said: 'The more I read him, the less I wonder that they poisoned him.'

On the arts, he opined: 'Perhaps no person can be a poet, or even enjoy poetry, without a certain unsoundness of mind.'

On a fellow politician: 'His imagination resembled the wings of an ostrich. It enabled him to run, though not to soar.'

Among his other quips, the following are worthy of note: 'I know of no spectacle so ridiculous as the British public in one of its periodical fits of morality.' And: 'Nothing is so useless as a general maxim.'

Fiery orator Daniel O'Connell was an extremely colourful character. On several occasions he was rather unwise to gripe to the press about his speeches not being given sufficient prominence and also about what he claimed was 'press misreporting'.

In the 1830s he complained again, on this occasion to *The Times*, saying: 'Your reporting is scandalous. I made a speech yesterday which was more cheered than any, I believe, I ever made. The report is contained in a few insignificant lines.' He went on to complain that those 'insignificant lines' were also incorrect. On this occasion, the journalist responsible unwisely tried to calm O'Connell by insisting that his notebook had got wet in the rain on the way back to his office and washed most of the words away. At this O'Connell erupted: 'That was the most extraordinary shower of rain I ever heard of, for it not only washed out the speech I made from your notebook, but it also washed in another and an entirely different one!' The ever-sensitive press corps imposed a ban on O'Connell as a result of his impudence, one journalist explaining that it was 'to repel with the utmost scorn and indignation the false and calumnious charges brought against us'.

Tory leader Arthur Balfour could have been talking about today's newspapers when musing over whether politicians should read them line by line. He concluded: 'I have never put myself to the trouble of rummaging through an immense rubbish heap on the problematical chance of discovering a cigar-end.'

He could have been talking about recent events in the Conservative Party when he said: 'It is not the principle of the Tory Party to stab its leaders in the back but I must confess it often appears to be a practice.'

Lord Dewar, who died in 1930, coined quite a few *bons mots*. Among his best are the following:

'The road to success is filled with women pushing their husbands along.'

'Four-fifths of the perjury in the world is expended on tombstones, women and competitors.'

'Lions of society are tigers for publicity.'

'Judge a man not by his clothes, but by his wife's clothes.'

'Love is an ocean of emotions, entirely surrounded by expenses.'

'A husband should tell his wife everything that he is sure she will find out, and before anyone else does.'

'Minds are like parachutes: they only function when open.'

'It is only the people with push who have a pull.'

And: 'Confessions may be good for the soul but they are bad for the reputation.'

Lloyd George, who was Britain's Prime Minister during the First World War, held public office for over seventeen years altogether. This impressive record has been recognized by politicians of all parties and Lloyd George is one of the few British statesmen who, along with Winston Churchill, has a statue erected in his honour in the Members' Lobby of the House of Commons.

He was a superb orator – an ability he retained right to the end of his life. He once said of a colleague he disliked: 'He is like the North Pole: often explored and never found.'

And, in a similar vein, he said of Lord Derby: 'He is like a cushion. He always bears the impression of the last man who sat on him.'

After listening to a fellow politician ranting at a public meeting, he remarked: 'It's easy to settle the problems of the world on a soap box.'

When a Cabinet colleague suggested caution, he snapped: Don't be afraid to take a big step if one is needed. You cannot cross a chasm in two small jumps.'

On Winston Churchill: 'He spoilt himself by reading about Napoleon.'

His comments on Tory MP Bonar Law also revealed something about his own make up, when he said: 'He was honest to the point of simplicity.'

His view of life as Prime Minister: 'There can be no friendship at the top.'

Tory Prime Minister Stanley Baldwin never expected to achieve the highest office in politics. Nor did many of his contemporaries. However, from the moment he entered Number 10 in 1923 until he quit active politics in 1937, he was a dominating influence in Britain. His impressive booming voice and down-to-earth approach made him, for a while, very popular with the public, although many of his Tory colleagues were irritated by his constant references to his humble origins and his pig farming.

Baldwin never liked or trusted Liberal politician Lloyd

George. When the latter was Chancellor of the Exchequer, he said of him: 'He is a mere shadow of his former self, wandering in a sort of Celtic twilight, his only intention being to rob hen roosts.'

And he later gave his own summary of Lloyd George's career: 'He spent his whole life in plastering together the true and the false and therefrom manufacturing the plausible.'

In 1933, Winston Churchill, then a back-bencher, was seeking to reverse the British government's policy on India and this set him on a collision course with Baldwin. Although not cordial, their relationship up till then, was at least amicable enough. Now, as a result of Churchill's campaigning, the two men no longer spoke to one another. One day, after leaving the chamber of the House of Commons, Churchill entered a small lavatory reserved for MPs which had only enough room for two men to relieve themselves at the same time. He saw, to his embarrassment, that one of the *pissoirs* was occupied by Baldwin. As Baldwin had noticed him entering, Churchill felt it was too late to retreat. Baldwin remained silent for a moment, then, as he did up his trousers, he turned to Churchill and snapped: 'I am glad that there is one common platform upon which we can still meet,' and walked off!

He later said of Churchill: 'He is a military adventurer who would sell his sword to anyone. He has his sentimental side but he lacks soul.'

However, he made his most effective swipe at Churchill in a public speech when he said: 'When Winston was born, lots of fairies swooped down on his cradle and gave him gifts – imagination, eloquence, industry and ability. Then came the fairy who said: "No one person has a right to so many gifts," picked him up and gave him a shake and a twist, and despite all these gifts, he was denied judgement and wisdom. And that is why, while we delight to listen to him in the House, we do not take his advice.'

Baldwin once quipped: 'The intelligent are to the intelligentsia what a gentleman is to the gents.'

Commenting on leading his party: 'Leading the Conservative Party is like driving pigs to market.'

And his view of socialism: 'No gospel founded on hate will ever be the gospel of our people.'

When he left office, Baldwin's popularity was as high as ever but the clouds of war gathering over Europe soon led to a change of public mood and, from 1940 onwards until his death, Baldwin was reviled for his earlier policy of appeasement. Upon his last day in office he did, however, make a remark to a passing journalist which is worth repeating and which even today is good advice for any retiring politician. He was asked whether, after leaving office, he would be available to give his successor the benefit of his opinions. He responded: 'No. Once I leave, I leave. I am not going to speak to the man on the bridge and I am not going to spit on the deck.'

Lord Curzon was a talented but arrogant politician who, even in his day, was regarded as somewhat out of touch. In an age when politicians were treated with deference by the press, he very nearly became Prime Minister. In the event, he lost out to Stanley Baldwin and he never quite came to terms with the fact.

Despite his disappointment, he agreed to serve as Baldwin's Foreign Secretary but showed little gratitude to his boss, of whom he remarked: 'It is heartbreaking serving under such a man. He is guilty of . . . a mixture of innocence, ignorance, honesty and stupidity – fatal gifts in a statesman when wholly dissociated from imagination, vision or *savoir faire*. He is a man of the utmost insignificance.'

On the Cabinet of which he was a member: 'They secretly grumble. Baldwin's evil geniuses are the whippersnappers of the Cabinet, Amery and Neville Chamberlain. They buzz about him day and night and he is lamentably weak.'

Former Labour premier Clement Attlee had an extremely terse style. He once shocked a TV news reporter to whom he had agreed to give an interview with his extremely laconic manner. The hapless reporter waited for his television colleagues to set up the recording equipment, the lights and the boom microphone and then began his great interview. 'Would the Prime Minister like to share with the viewers his plans for the forthcoming General Election?' he asked.

Attlee puffed on his pipe: 'No,' he replied. 'Next question.'

Perhaps this behaviour was partly because he had a dim view of television, later describing it as 'an idiot's lantern.'

He gave his opinion of communism, describing it as 'the illegitimate child of Karl Marx and Catherine the Great.'

After he quit the Commons, he took his seat in the House of Lords, as by custom most Prime Ministers do. He soon noticed the different atmosphere saying: 'The House of Lords is like a glass of champagne that has stood for five days.'

Sir Winston Churchill, one of only three recent premiers not to take a seat in the House of Lords,* was the master of the political insult. During sixty-two years in the House

---

* The others are Sir Edward Heath MP, Prime Minister 1970-74, who has chosen to remain in the Commons, and John Major, Prime Minister 1990-1997, who has yet to decide his future, but currently remains an MP.

of Commons, his humour and wit enlivened many a debate and his sharp tongue put down many an opponent.

It is well known that it is out of order for one MP to call another 'a liar' in the House of Commons. Churchill cleverly managed to do so, within the rules of order, by referring to the remarks of an opponent as being a 'terminological inexactitude'.

His view of Mr Attlee, the Labour Party leader, is well known: "An empty taxi cab drew up at the House of Commons and Clement Attlee got out."

After his capture in the Boer War, he joined the South African Light Horse and grew a moustache. A friend of his mother said she neither cared for his politics nor his moustache. Churchill replied: 'Madam, I see no earthly reason why you should come into contact with either.'

On Labour Prime Minister Ramsay MacDonald: 'He has, more than any other man, the gift of compressing the largest number of words into the smallest amount of thought.'

Churchill on Bonar Law, when the latter was leader of the Conservative Party and Churchill was still a Liberal: 'The raw and rowdy Under-Secretary* whom the nakedness of the land and the jealousies of his betters have promoted to the leadership of the Tory Party.'

On Communist Russia: 'I cannot forecast to you the action of Russia. It is a riddle wrapped in a mystery inside an enigma.'

On the qualities required for political office: 'In my belief, you cannot deal with the most serious things in the world unless you also understand the most amusing.'

---

* Bonar Law, although leader of the Tories in opposition, had never been more than a junior minister when the party was in office.

On Sir William Joynson-Hicks MP, former Home Secretary: 'The worst that can be said of him is that he runs the risk of being most humorous when he wishes to be most serious.'

On Communism: 'The foul baboonery of Bolshevism.'

His view of the Labour Government's foreign policy: 'Dreaming all night of giving away bits of the British Empire, and spending all day doing it!'

His definition of a prisoner of war: 'Someone who tries to kill you, fails and then asks you not to kill him.'

Commenting on Sir Redvers Buller, commander-in-chief of the British forces during the Boer War: 'He was a characteristic British personality. He looked stolid. He said little and what he said was obscure. He was a man of considerable scale. He plodded on from blunder to blunder and from one disaster to another, without losing either the regard of his country or the trust of his troops, to whose feeding as well as his own he paid serious attention.'

And, on the Sudanese soldier: 'At once slovenly and uxorious, he detested his drills and loved his wives with equal earnestness.'

When a cabbage was thrown at him while he was speaking at a public meeting, he showed his ready wit with the riposte: 'I asked for the gentleman's ears, not his head.'

Although he insulted many, including some women, he expressed his philosophy on the opposite sex: 'It is hard, if not impossible, to snub a beautiful woman; they remain beautiful and the snub rebounds.'

On an official report he received from Admiral Pound, who Churchill did not rate, he wrote in the margin: 'Pennywise.'

After an election defeat, he said: 'I returned with feelings of deflation which a bottle of champagne represents when it is half-emptied and left uncorked for a night.'

On fellow Tory, Stanley Baldwin: 'An epileptic corpse. Occasionally he stumbled over the truth, but hastily picked himself up and hurried on as if nothing had happened.'

After Adolf Hitler had militarized the Rhineland, he attacked Premier Baldwin's unpreparedness: 'The Government simply cannot make up their minds, or they cannot get the Prime Minister to make up his mind. So they go on in strange paradox, decided only to be undecided, resolved to be irresolute, adamant for drift, solid for fluidity, all powerful to be impotent.'

During the war, a senior naval officer complained that his service's role in the conflict was not in accordance with its great traditions. 'Well, Admiral, have you ever asked yourself what the traditions of the Royal Navy are?' Churchill asked. 'I will tell you in three words: rum, sodomy and the lash.'

As he first became Prime Minister during the Second World War, it is not surprising that a number of Churchill's barbs were directed at Adolf Hitler. He said of the German leader: 'I always hate to compare Napoleon with Hitler, as it seems an insult to the great Emperor and warrior to connect him in any way with a squalid caucus boss and butcher.'

On Hitler's tactics: 'When a snake wants to eat his victims he first covers them with saliva.'

On Prime Minister Neville Chamberlain's attempts to agree peace with Hitler: 'You were given the choice between war and dishonour. You chose dishonour and you will have war.'

On dictators generally, he said: 'Dictators ride to and fro upon tigers which they dare not dismount.'

When Germany invaded Czechoslovakia after the Munich Agreement, Prime Minister Neville Chamberlain complained that he could not imagine anyone lying to him, claiming he had been betrayed by Hitler. Churchill opined: 'This high belief in the perfection of man is appropriate in a man of the cloth, but not in a Prime Minister.'

His comment on the policies of Lenin: 'Christianity with a tomahawk.'

When it was announced that Tom Driberg, the left-wing Labour MP, was to marry, quite a few eyebrows were raised. Driberg's homosexuality was well known at Westminster, and when a photograph of the MP with his extremely plain fiancée appeared in one of the daily papers, Churchill was heard to say: 'Ah well, buggers can't be choosers.' On hearing this a fellow MP added: 'Poor woman – she won't know which way to turn.'

On F. E. Smith MP, before they became friends: 'No one has succeeded in manufacturing a greater amount of heroism with a smaller consumption of the raw material of danger.'

On Lord Charles Beresford: 'He can best be described as one of those orators who, before they get up, do not know what they are going to say; when they are speaking, do not know what they are saying; and when they have sat down, do not know what they have said.'

On Lord Rosebery: 'He outlived his future by ten years and his past by more than twenty.'

On the House of Lords: 'The House of Lords is not a national institution but a party dodge.'

To George Wyndham MP, in a debate in the Commons: 'I like the martial and commanding air with which the Right Honourable Gentleman treats facts. He stands no nonsense from them.'

On a former Conservative MP seeking to stand as a Liberal: 'The only instance of a rat swimming towards a sinking ship.'*

He frequently railed against the BBC saying it was an organization that was 'honeycombed with socialists – probably with communists', and on one memorable occasion he exploded when the BBC Director-General John (later Lord) Reith insisted that broadcasts during the General Strike of 1926 had to be 'impartial'. He considered this outrageous and told Reith: 'You have no right to be impartial between the fire and the fire brigade.'

Once, after being attacked by his opponents, he replied with gusto: 'Nothing in life is more exhilarating than to be shot at without result.'

In reply to criticism that he was scaring the public with his speeches about the dangers of the Nazi regime: 'It is much better to be frightened now than to be killed hereafter.'

His view of politics generally: 'A politician is asked to stand, he wants to sit and he is expected to lie.'

Brushing aside an attack by Ulster MP James Craig: 'If I valued his opinion I might get angry.'

When a young MP told a rather vulgar joke in his presence, Churchill quipped: 'Young man, I predict you will go far – in the wrong direction.'

Upon being told that an arrest had been made in Hyde Park involving a semi-naked man who had been making sexual advances to another in sub-zero temperature, his reaction was: 'Naked and below zero! Makes you proud to be British.'

---

* This barb was re-used very successfully over thirty years later by Nigel Lawson, who said of the announcement by the Liberals in the 1970s that they were to form the Lib–Lab pact with the then Labour government: 'The only time in history that rats have joined a sinking ship.'

The following are among his best quips: 'Never prophesy unless you know.'

'Too often the strong, silent man is silent because he does not know what to say.'

'Never be afraid to eat your words. On the whole I have found them to be a most wholesome diet.'

'The longer you can look back, the farther you can look forward.'

Reflecting on his life in politics he said: 'In war you can only be killed once but in politics you can be killed many times.'

And, on himself: 'Megalomania is the only form of sanity.'

French President Charles de Gaulle's view of politicians: 'Since a politician never believes what he says, he is surprised when others believe him.'

De Gaulle also said: 'When I am right, I get angry. Churchill gets angry when he is wrong. So we were very often angry at each other.'

Labour heavyweight Aneurin Bevan was once asked by a new MP, 'How do you choose your friends in the House of Commons?' He replied: 'You don't have to worry about choosing your friends here – it is choosing your enemies that matters.'

Bevan was one of the most effective Labour debaters of his day. During and just after the Second World War, no one could match his great gift of oratory. However, his weakness was his acerbic tongue and he would often cross the line between robust argument and unacceptable invective. In the 1940s he caused uproar when he said: 'No amount of cajolery and no attempt at ethical and social seduction can eradicate from my heart a deep burning hatred for the Tory Party . . . in so far as I am concerned, they are lower than vermin.'

Of his own party leader, Clement Attlee: 'He seems determined to make a trumpet sound like a tin whistle. He brings to the fierce struggle of politics the tepid enthusiasm of a lazy summer afternoon at a cricket match.'

When Tory Prime Minister Harold Macmillan sacked a number of his ministers in a reshuffle, one of those he dismissed, Lord Kilmuir, complained that 'a cook would have been given more notice of his dismissal'. Macmillan shot back: 'Ah, but good cooks are hard to find.'

Commenting on a colleague: 'He is forever poised between a cliché and an indiscretion.'

Macmillan summed up much of parliamentary badinage when he said: 'I have never found, in a long experience of politics, that criticism is ever inhibited by ignorance.'

Showing signs of irritation in the early 1960s when the then leader of the Labour Party, Harold Wilson, claimed to the press that, when he was a boy, his family were too poor to afford to buy him any boots, Macmillan snapped: 'If Harold Wilson ever went to school without any boots, it was merely because he was too big for them.'

Richard Austen Butler, known universally as 'Rab', twice almost became Prime Minister, but was regarded as too left-wing by many mainstream Conservatives, some of whom openly referred to him as 'a milk and water socialist'. His critics also claimed that he behaved more like a civil servant than a politician. Beyond dispute was his undoubted talent for organizing and management; what was questioned was his vision and his willingness to stand up to civil servants and political opponents.

He preferred to make out a good case for what he was doing, choosing to ignore the political barb and insult. The result was usually that his speeches were well argued but lacked punch.

Despite his generally quiet manner, he did sometimes resort to the discomfiting comment and even occasionally 'put the boot in'. When a right-wing Conservative showed he was unconcerned about the effects of economic deflation, he retorted: 'Those like you who talk about creating pools of unemployment should be thrown into them and made to swim.'

His view of Lord Beaverbrook was succinct: 'I found him green and apish.'

Of Labour Premier Harold Wilson he opined: 'He was adept at using the smear as a political weapon.'

On Sir Samuel Hoare MP, former Secretary of State for India: 'I was amazed by his ambitions; I admired his imagination, I stood in awe of his intellectual capacity, but I was never touched by his humanity. He was the coldest fish with whom I ever had to deal.'

On former Prime Minister Sir Alec Douglas-Home, who became leader of the Conservative Party in 1963, when many thought Rab would be chosen: 'An amiable enough creature – however, I am afraid he doesn't understand economics or even education at all.'

Later, taking a further swipe at Sir Alec, with just a hint of bitterness, he added: 'I may never have known much about ferrets or flower arranging, but one thing I did know is how to govern the people of this country.'

He was invited to attend the retirement dinner of Lord Fraser of Kilmorach. He declined, adding: 'There is no one I would rather attend a farewell dinner for than Lord Fraser.' Even those who knew him could not be sure whether he meant to be insulting, but offence was taken at the remark.

In a similar vein, when he was Master of Trinity College, he said to a retiring clerk of works: 'My wife and I are glad to have got here in time to see you leave.' The clerk was deeply offended.

During the early part of Sir Anthony Eden's premiership – before the Suez fiasco – some newspapers began to speculate on Eden's future. Caught at Heathrow Airport by a journalist who invited him to comment on the press reports, Rab uttered what was to become his most famous remark. When asked whether he supported Eden, he replied: 'Well, he is the best Prime Minister we have.'

Some political commentators thought such remarks were uttered quite innocently, but those who knew him well believed differently. Indeed, some of his friends thought that this waspish irreverence helped to prevent him from becoming leader of the Conservative Party, a view supported by Professor Galbraith who has said that it was Rab's habit of looking on others with 'ill-concealed amusement' that stopped him from reaching the very top.

Although many Tories in the country felt he was unfairly denied the premiership, this view was by no means unanimous in the parliamentary party. During the war, the Conservative MP for Chichester, Major J. S. Courtauld, said of him: 'He's industrious but loopy.'

Charles Parnell once observed: 'In politics, the plural of conscience is too often conspiracy.'

Harold (later Lord) Wilson is the most successful leader the Labour Party has had. He led his party to victory in the general elections of 1964, 1966 and (just) 1974, failing only once in 1970 when he lost to Ted Heath.

A significant element of Wilson's success was his ability to manage the Labour Party effectively and, in the main, prevent damaging splits between the left and right wings from emerging. Wilson had the knack of papering over the cracks, and candidly admitted how he did it: 'Leading the Labour Party is like driving an old stage coach. If it is rattling along at a rare old speed, most of the passengers are so exhilarated – perhaps even seasick – they don't start arguing or quarrel-ling. As soon as it stops, they start arguing about which way to go. The trick is to keep it going at an exhilarating speed.'

Wilson's preoccupation with keeping Labour together soon led his detractors to accuse him of pursuing expediency rather than formulated policy. Indeed, it might be said that the views he expressed on the Tory statesman Benjamin Disraeli could equally apply to his own career. Of Disraeli he commented: 'He had a complete and almost proverbial lack of political principle, often acting by instinct.'

Wilson's view on Ramsay MacDonald, Labour's first Prime Minister: 'He still embodies a legend of betrayal to the Labour Party, without having secured a word of tribute. He gradually became a pathetic figure, tired, ill, rambling and taking refuge in virtually meaningless and almost unending phrases.'

He also made less than complimentary comments on the following:

On Stanley Baldwin: 'He was the antithesis of Lloyd George. He would conduct the orchestra and not tire himself. He was the finely tuned manipulator of the steering wheel: direction without engine power, the prerogative of the bosun throughout the ages.'

On Baldwin's successor, Tory PM Neville Chamberlain: 'It was not only that he was totally inadequate as Prime Minister: many are and some get by. What was tragic was that he was totally opinionated, totally certain he was right.'

He had a poor opinion of Britain's nineteenth-century Prime Minister Lord Aberdeen: 'As a leader he was weak and unfit for the premiership.'

Wilson on the Liberal Party at the end of the last century: 'Gladstone clung to the leadership and an increasingly rebellious party simply did not dare get rid of him. No one would bell the cat.'

On Herbert Morrison, who served in Clement Attlee's Labour Cabinet: 'He was not so much disloyal as watching for a favourable opportunity to be disloyal.'

On former Tory PM Sir Anthony Eden: 'He was one of the great gentlemen of British politics – and one of the great tragedies. He had a jealous temperament.'

His view of his former adversary, Conservative Prime Minister Harold (later Lord) Macmillan: 'Macmillan's role as a poseur was itself a pose. He was a patrician in a non-patrician age, a dedicated professional who gave the impression of effortless government. He was one of the most articulate of Britain's premiers who regarded the premiership as a source of continuous enjoyment. He was a Disraelian, perhaps the last Disraelian Prime Minister Britain will see.'

Perhaps his most effective put-down of Macmillan was the barb: 'He had an expensive education - Eton and Suez.'

With the Suez crisis in mind, Wilson later opined: 'One of the laws of politics is that nothing provocative must be allowed to occur in an allied country in the year leading up to an American presidential election.'

On former Labour Chancellor of the Exchequer Hugh Dalton: 'Apart from his loud voice, he had little to commend him. He had an infinite capacity for meeting himself coming back.'

On political power: 'Every statesman should remember his power to evoke a reaction-coefficient greater than unity.'

His view of the qualities required of a Prime Minister: 'No one should attempt the role of Prime Minister who cannot fall asleep the moment he is in bed with the cares and worries of the day behind him.'

Defending his own approach to the role of Prime Minister: 'A healer does not usually get a good press. Fleet Street thrives on confrontation. If a Prime Minister uses his political skills to keep the Cabinet together in pursuit of a common aim and common policies, he is condemned as devious; if he forces splits and public recriminations then, as long as he takes the right side in the division, he is a hero - but his Cabinet disintegrates.'

On P. G. Wodehouse: 'He had a naïve insistence on visiting Hitler's Berlin and broadcasting unpatriotic claptrap on their radio during the war.'

Throughout most of Wilson's time at Number 10, he faced Ted Heath as leader of the Opposition, about whom he said: 'A shiver looking for a spine to run up.'

Early in 1972 there was a political row when unemployment passed the one million mark. Wilson, at this time, was in Opposition and the Prime Minister was Edward Heath. Heath had just returned from the EU negotiations (then called the EEC) in Brussels, which led Wilson to gibe: 'Heath is the first dole queue millionaire to cross the channel since Neville Chamberlain.'

Back in power after the 1974 general election, Wilson faced a difficult public expenditure round with a slender parliamentary majority. In the vote, a number of left-wing Labour MPs abstained, which caused the Labour government to lose the motion on public expenditure. Some defended their action by saying that they could have voted with the Conservatives, but didn't. Wilson, who was furious, snapped, 'It is always an arguable question about promiscuity whether one is more open to criticism for going into the bedroom or being the lap dog outside the door.'

He later referred to the comfort that the Labour left-wingers had given to the Conservatives as 'An unholy parliamentary alliance that can only be described as arsenic and red chiffon.'

On his then Industry Minister, Tony Benn: 'Tony has some of the qualities of an Old Testament prophet without the beard. He rambles on about the new Jerusalem.'

When the economic difficulties of the late 1960s caused Wilson's popularity to plummet, an anonymous insulting letter started to circulate in political and show-biz circles, claiming to be from the hitherto unknown 'Harold Wilson Memorial Fund of London'. I remember that I was one of those sent a copy.

At the time, the amusing missive was also received by some of my friends. I am most grateful to one of the dearest of these, the British ventriloquist Arthur Worsley, who still retains this epistle and who has recently enabled me to refresh my memory therefrom.

The letter reads:

The Harold Wilson Memorial Fund, London

We have the distinguished honour of being members of this committee to raise five million pounds to place a statue of Mr Harold Wilson in front of the Houses of Parliament.

The Committee is in a quandary in selecting the proper location for the statue. It was thought not wise to place it beside the statue of George Washington, who never told a lie, nor beside that of Lloyd George, who never told the truth, since Harold Wilson can never tell the difference.

After careful consideration we thought it would be a good idea to place it beside the statue of Christopher Columbus, the greatest Socialist of them all, in that he started out not knowing where he was going, on arrival did not know where he was, and on returning did not know where he had been – and he did it all on borrowed money!

Moses said to the children of Israel, 'Pick up your shovels, mount your asses and camels and I will lead you to the Promised Land.' Some two thousand years later, Frank Cousins* said, 'Lay down your shovels, sit on your asses, light a Camel – this is the Promised Land.' And now Harold Wilson is stealing your shovels, kicking your asses, raising the price of Camels and taking over the Promised Land.

If you are a citizen of this Promised Land with any money left after paying taxes and meeting rising costs, please make a generous contribution to this worthwhile project.

Yours faithfully,

The Committee

Despite Wilson's considerable success in keeping Labour in power, his former Cabinet colleague Richard Crossman was

* Trade Unionist. General Secretary of TGWU 1956-1969.

not impressed: 'Harold Wilson had one overriding aim – to remain in office. He would use almost every trick or gimmick to achieve it. Whenever I go to see Harold, I look into those grey eyes – and see nothing.'

The late Labour MP Bessie Braddock, often the butt of gibes herself, said of former Labour Cabinet member, Richard Crossman: 'He is a man of many opinions – most of them of short duration.'

The colourful Tory back-bencher, the late Sir Gerald Nabarro, was never off our television screens in the 1960s, usually insulting one or other of his parliamentary contemporaries – usually one of his own party colleagues.

Of Labour MP Albert Murray he was dismissive: 'The man is a mere flatulent lightweight.'

Commenting on a speech by his own Chancellor of the Exchequer, Harold Macmillan: 'I was captivated by the Chancellor's reply on the fourth of December, and I have been poring over it ever since. I have been trying to determine exactly what he meant.'

On the attitudes of British management in the 1950s and 60s: 'In the post-war world in Britain it has been considered in many circles to be slightly off to be eager, slightly improper to be thrusting, not done to be ambitious. Quite simply, these sentiments are drivel.'

Once, seeing a middle-aged member of the public using a telephone reserved for MPs, Nabarro grabbed the man by the scruff of the neck, beckoned a policeman and bellowed: 'These phones are reserved for use by MPs only,' demanding

that the officer throw the miscreant out of the building. 'But
this is Hugh McCartney,' the officer explained, who at that
time was a Labour Member of Parliament. Unabashed, Nabarro
walked off yelling: 'Well, he's never bloody here anyway.'

Not long after Nabarro's death, two Tory MPs were discussing him in the Members' Smoking Room of the House of
Commons: 'The man was a complete shit,' said the first. This
drew the riposte from the other: 'There is no need to be nice
to him now he is dead.'

Harold Wilson's Deputy Prime Minister was, for a time,
George Brown, the able but unpredictable and somewhat
neurotic Labour MP for Belper in Derbyshire. His unpre-
dictability increased in direct proportion to his intake of
alcohol.

He served Wilson as Secretary of State for Economic Affairs
and later as Foreign Secretary. When he was upset about
some issue he started to make a habit of threatening to resign
from the government. All in all he threatened eight
resignations, once of the grounds of a row with his own wife!

Wilson usually handled these threats with a great deal of tact,
but not always. Once, when Brown in a highly agitated state
stormed out of a meeting he was having with Wilson, the
Prime Minister waited and as expected Brown later returned
to the discussions. Brown raised a particular issue and Wilson
retorted that now that the sixteenth resignation was out of
the way, they could discuss matters further 'when the
occasion was reached for the seventeenth'. At this Brown
blew up and again stormed out of the deliberations.

When his Labour colleagues were privately debating the
merits of the Sexual Offenders Bill, which relaxed the laws
on homosexuality, Brown exploded, becoming extremely

agitated and aggressive. He started insulting homosexuals and the prevailing tolerant attitude towards them. 'Society ought to have higher standards,' he bellowed. 'If this Bill gets through we will have a totally disorganized, indecent and unpleasant society. We've gone too far on sex already.' Then, to the astonishment of those present, he added: 'I don't regard sex as pleasant. It's pretty undignified and I've always thought so.' His last remarks raised quite a few eyebrows, particularly as Brown frequently went through the far more undignified process of being publicly drunk, on one occasion falling into the gutter and on another smashing his car into a wall in the precincts of the Commons.

One story, oft-repeated at Westminster, relates to Brown's attendance at a reception hosted by the President of Austria. Just before canapés were served, a band struck up and Brown, then Foreign Secretary, asked a figure dressed in scarlet to dance with him. The figure replied: 'There are three reasons why I will not dance with you. First, you are drunk. Secondly, this is not a dance but my country's national anthem and thirdly, I am the Cardinal Archbishop of Vienna.'

Despite all this, he still had his fans. During this period *The Times* remarked that 'George Brown drunk is a better man than the Prime Minister [Wilson] sober.'

He resigned from the government for the final time in March 1968 over Wilson's style of leadership. Although it is reported the he later tried to see Wilson to effect a reconciliation, Wilson, who had clearly had enough, went to ground and the eighth resignation was allowed to take effect.

Brown was sent to the Lords but he did not much care for the experience. He gradually fell out with most of his Labour colleagues and, towards the end of his life, resigned once more, this time from the Labour Party itself in 1976. Commenting later on Labour leader Michael Foot he opined: 'The Labour Party should not be led by someone who has one eye and one leg.' One of Foot's friends, alluding to Brown's legendary drinking, dismissed Brown's outburst with the riposte: 'In the country of the legless, the one-legged man is king.'

Reginald Paget, the former Labour MP, had a fruity metaphor for Tory Prime Minister Sir Anthony Eden, saying: 'He's like an over-ripe banana – yellow outside and squishy inside.'

Author and former Tory MP Sir Julian Critchley was always worth listening to in debate. His speeches were witty and invariably peppered with insults.

On his own Party: 'The Conservative Party in the House of Commons contains the party conference of ten years ago. Cheerful girls in hats who once moved motions in favour of corporal and capital punishment on behalf of the Young Conservatives of some Midlands town, small-town solicitors and estate-agents with flat provincial accents are now its members. As Mrs Thatcher went up in the world, so the Party came down.'

On Norman (now Lord) Tebbit: 'He was the rude child saying that the Emperor had no clothes. He didn't just say it – he shouted it from the rooftops. If he had entered politics a decade earlier, the Conservative Party would have been embarrassed by him but to the Thatcherites he was a hero. But he did not last long in government after the 1987 election. Like Dick Whittington, he turned again and made for the City.'

And commenting on Mr Tebbit's ennoblement: 'He should have taken the title "The Prince of Darkness".'

On tabloid columnist John Juror: 'That unamiable old Scot.'

On former Labour leader Michael Foot: 'That distinguished old man of letters gave the impression of being no more at home in 1980s politics than Soames Forsyte would have been had he been dropped into a City office full of yuppies.'

On Neil Kinnock: 'Effective Opposition calls for a degree of subtlety and certainly for careful research to get the facts right. That was scarcely Neil's way. He was happier when getting to his feet, working himself into a peak of righteous indignation, and belting it out.'

On Jeffrey (now Lord) Archer: 'He was not a serious politician. But his footwork should command respect. He is proof of the proposition that in each of us lurks one bad novel.'

On the late Robert Maxwell, who was once a Labour MP: 'Maxwell was the bad taste in the mouth but his zeal was unquestionable. The Bouncing Czech had resilience.'

On back-bench Old Labour MPs: 'Public-bar abuse is the stock-in-trade of the rougher end of the Labour Party.'

His view of government office: 'Junior ministers are chauffeur-driven into obscurity, reappearing once a month at question time in order to read out replies prepared beforehand by some Wykehamist.'

On his long-time friend Michael Heseltine: 'He tends not to be able to see a parapet without ducking below it.'

On the former Tory MP Peter Bruinvels: 'He is beyond satire.'

During Mrs T's premiership he said of her: 'If she has a weakness it is for shopkeepers, which probably accounts for the fact that she cannot pass a branch of Marks and Spencer without inviting the manager to join her private office. In the party, the Military Cross has given way to Rotary Club badges. The Knights of the Shires have given way to estate agents and accountants.'

And on his own reason for entering politics: 'I became a Tory not from conviction, but from pleasure.'

The late Labour peer and columnist **Lord Wyatt** had a colourful turn of phrase. On his party's former premier Jim Callaghan: 'He was skilful in debate, persuasive in speech – and disastrous at his job.'

On politicians: 'A good character is not merely unnecessary for becoming Prime Minister – it may be positively harmful.'

On the House of Commons: 'The House listens with great humility to humbugs and compliments them on their sincerity. It hates to hear awkward truths and abuses those who tell them. It suffers fools, particularly sentimental ones, gladly.'

Sir Nicholas Fairbairn was, in his day, a first-rate lawyer and politician. His entries in *Who's Who*, mentioned below, were always worth reading and his Commons performances, except perhaps towards the end, could be nothing short of brilliant. I frequently enjoyed his acerbic company in the Members' Smoking Room of the House of Commons, where he delighted in ridiculing and insulting anyone and everyone who passed by his table.

He was in every sense a colourful politician known among other things for his somewhat eccentric taste in clothes. He was often seen around the House wearing tartan trousers and unusual jackets, which he designed himself. He was extremely forthright in expressing his views and possessed a highly caustic tongue, making it an extremely dangerous pastime to cross swords with this former Scottish law officer.

In the last couple of years of his life, however, he became extremely unreliable and was frequently the worse for drink. When he told me that he was writing the final part of his autobiography, I expected him to announce that the book was going to be called *The Wrath of Grapes*.

He was, particularly towards the end of his life, a bane of his own party's whips' office and always loudly referred to his own regional whip, Timothy Kirkhope MP, as 'Mothy'. Although many colleagues found him exasperating, the impish grin and the boyish twinkle in his eye caused many he had offended to forgive him readily even though he usually reserved his fiercest criticisms for members of his own party.

On one of his last visits to the Commons he nearly caused a riot at the Members' Entrance. Waiting for a taxi, he approached an extremely attractive young woman in evening dress. She was an MP's wife and had just arrived to meet her husband to attend an evening function. Fairbairn, who had never seen her before, approached. 'Good evening, my dear. You are very pretty. And what a beautiful dress.' So far so good. Then he decided to try his luck. 'However, can I offer some advice. I have to say you would look *far more* beautiful if you took the dress off. Can I help you in this regard?' Luckily, the policeman on duty ushered him off into a cab before the astonished woman had time to react.

On former Prime Minister John Major he expressed a low opinion: 'More a ventriloquist's dummy than a Prime Minister.'

On Tories Kenneth Clarke and Michael Heseltine: 'I don't like Clarke and I don't trust Heseltine - Clarke's a bounder and Heseltine's a spiv.'

On Willie (now Lord) Whitelaw, he was vicious: 'He is the living person I most despise because he represents what I despise most - sanctimony, guile, slime and intrigue under a cloak of decency, all for self-advancement – it's called hypocrisy.'

Among his other most memorable utterances were the following:

On Sarah, Duchess of York: 'She is a lady short on looks, absolutely deprived of any dress sense, has a figure like a Jurassic monster, is very greedy when it comes to loot, has no tact, and wants to upstage everyone else.'

When, during a speaking engagement at Edinburgh University, a young female student had the temerity to mock his outfit, he retorted: 'You are a silly, rude bitch and since you are a potential breeder, God help the next generation.'

When referring to another member in the House of Commons, MPs are not permitted to call each other by name, but need to refer to the constituency of the MP concerned. During a rather heated debate, Labour's Frank Dobson, the MP for Holborn and St Pancras, found himself the subject of Fairbairn's ire. Fairbairn, adding insult to injury, referred to Dobson as 'The MP for the two tube stations.'

Asked about electoral law during the 1992 general election, he opined: 'Why should the bastard child of an American sailor serving in Dunoon have a vote in Scotland even though he's in America, when the legitimate son of a Gordon Highlander born in Daarnstadt who's resident in Carlisle has no vote or say in Scotland?'

A few years ago during a debate in Committee Sir Nicholas crossed swords with the former Labour MP, the late Norman Buchan. Mr Buchan was becoming quite excited during the debate on an amendment to the Criminal Justice Bill, arguing that no lawyer should in future have to wear a gown 'or a uniform of any kind'. Mr Buchan went somewhat over the top claiming that the purpose of all uniform and dress was merely to identify the office of the wearer. This was too much for Sir Nicholas who silenced him with: 'If that's what he thinks, why does the Honourable Member wear trousers? Is it in order to have a crutch for his dignity – or to protect the dignity of his crutch?'

On former Scottish Labour MP Dennis Canavan he remarked: 'I take the view that he, who knows more about madness than anyone else, should continue his career as a merchant of discourtesy elsewhere.'

He once told a journalist: 'I was born the year that Hitler came to power, although he wasn't as good a painter as I am.'

On further European integration: 'Attempts to make Europe right and pure by being nice to those who want to divide it in their own interests won't work. All being called Schmidt and speaking Esperanto is not the way ahead.'

On John Major's Citizen's Charter: 'The concept's good, but it's wishy-washy and just another opportunity for bureaucratic officiousness.'

Although he generally supported John Major's government, Fairbairn did not like Major's idea of a 'classless society', commenting: 'What is it? Just a ridiculous phrase.'

While he was serving as Solicitor-General for Scotland he was once asked by the Scottish Labour MP John Maxton if he appreciated that the 'alarming spread of glue-sniffing among 14- and 15-year-olds is due to the lack of employment, caused by his government, and their consequent sense of uselessness.' Fairbairn swatted him with the rebuff: 'Glue-sniffing is not a habit normally indulged in by children above the age of 16. It is a criminal offence to employ a child below that age. But if glue-sniffing induces a sense of uselessness, it amazes me that the Honourable Member has not taken up the habit himself.'

In 1988 the salmonella crisis resulted in the resignation of

Junior Health Minister Edwina Currie. Afterwards, during a routine debate Mr Fairbairn interrupted Edwina's speech with the barb: 'Does the Honourable Lady remember that she was an egg herself once; and very many members of all sides of this House regret that it was ever fertilized?' Vicious!

His view of marriage shocked many of his colleagues: 'Christian monogamy and its assumption of fidelity is as fallacious as the Catholic concept of the chastity of priests. I am sure that polygamy and harems probably worked better. We live in a priggish and prim age.'

And when asked what were the attractions (if any) of marriage he replied: 'Apart from the depth of the relationship, you remember when you turn over in bed who you're with – and you don't have to get up at dawn and get out.'

Upsetting in one swoop all women MPs, just before his death he said: 'They don't give me feelings of femininity. They lack fragrance. They're definitely not desert island material. They all look as though they're from the 5th Kiev Stalinist machine-gun parade. As for Edwina Currie – well the only person who smells her fragrance is herself. I can't stand the hag.'

When fellow Tory MP Patrick Cormack attacked Sir Nicholas and referred to his 'eccentric and ridiculous utterances, bad manners and eccentric garb', Fairbairn said of Cormack: 'His manners are always appalling and his dress sense is worse. He is a squit.'

Sir Nicholas had a long-running line in insults against former Prime Minister Sir Edward Heath. This being so it came as quite a surprise when the press revealed that Sir Nicholas had sent a letter to Ted congratulating him on becoming a Knight of the Garter. Of this incident Fairbairn said: 'The *Daily Telegraph* has said that while one could be rude to one's friends in private, one should be polite to them in public. Well, that's the contrary to all I was brought up to believe. To write and rejoice in what was clearly for him a reason for great satisfaction for himself was the proper thing to do. But then, why can't I say he was a dreadful Prime Minister and his public behaviour appalling? The fact that he sent my private letter to the press shows he has no manners. He has grave personality problems and torment within himself which he'll never resolve.'

And warming to this theme he added: 'To him chivalry is unknown. Since the Order of the Garter arose out of an incident in which a man of little rank despised a lady of great standing, what could be more fitting?'

On former Defence Minister Alan Clark: 'A rich goon with perverted views.'

He was always generous of insult but less so when it came to handing out praise. When I suggested to him that F. E. Smith (later first Earl of Birkenhead) was a great lawyer, he was dismissive: 'Not a bad lawyer. But not great. In fact I am much better.' And he meant it.

He frequently changed the list of his own recreations in *Who's Who*. He initially listed these as: 'Making love, ends meet and people laugh.' This was then changed to: 'Draining brains and scanning bodies.' In 1990 his entry became: 'Growling, prowling, scowling and owling.' Finally, just before his death, he changed his list to read: 'Drawing ships, making quips, confounding whips and scuttling drips.'

After a particularly colourful insult by Sir Nicholas a Tory backbench MP was overheard to remark: 'He is in his element again – hot water.'

The late Labour MP Bob Cryer was one of the banes of the Conservative Party Whips' office. During Mrs Thatcher's time

in office, he would frequently debate at length the uncontro-
versial Money Resolution to a bill or give the House the
benefit of his views on a Ways and means Resolution, merely
to keep Conservative MPs up at a late hour. He would do this
especially if his own party had agreed that there should be no
debate or delay, commenting: 'Consensus in the chamber is
the worst aspect of Parliament at work.' It was a testament to
his parliamentary skills that this filibustering was always
entirely within the rules of order.

He would also frequently divide the House even when his
own party had decided not to. On politics generally he
commented: 'One of the problems of democracy is that we
can never be sure of the outcome.'

Of the House of Commons he said: 'One of the strengths of
the Commons is that it is awkward.' By his own definition,
Bob Cryer added to those strengths. His untimely death in a
car accident robbed the House of a great parliamentarian.

Politicians are usually accused by the press and the public
of not being candid enough. Such an accusation could certainly not be levelled against former Tory MP Sir John Foster
if his 'off the record' comments are anything to go by.

Once he was being interviewed by Granada Television and
gave a rather reactionary and patriotic response to the
interviewer's questions. After the recording was over, Sir
John astounded the interviewer by saying: 'By the way, you
ought to know that my public pronouncements bear no
relation to my private views and there are three things I
cannot stand – God, the Queen and the family.'

The House of Commons lost an intellect of the highest calibre when veteran politician Enoch Powell was defeated in the 1987 general election. On his death in 1998 generous tributes were made by politicians of all parties, although memories of his notorious 'rivers of blood' speech made in the 60s still caused some commentators to portray him unfairly as a right-wing bigot.

Throughout his political life, any controversy he caused was usually as a direct result of his honesty. Enoch would always articulate his fears, concerns or conclusions, reached after he had logically considered the issue under discussion. However, brutal candour can create enemies and is not always a wise course for a democratic politician to take. Sometimes, a little blarney and diplomacy are necessary sweeteners when the message is unpalatable.

Once, when a supporter told him that 'The world would be a better place with more people like you,' his reaction was typical. Most politicians would respond with some grateful small talk, saying 'I am only doing my job,' or 'I appreciate your support,' but not Enoch. He reflected on the proposition that had just been made and gave his conclusion: 'No, I disagree,' he began, astonishing his fan. Then he explained his reasoning to the by now incredulous disciple: 'A society for survival needs a spread of types. For example, in every battalion there's one man who deserves the VC, and one man who ought to be shot for cowardice. The battalion depends for its success upon a spectrum connecting those two.' Leaving the man speechless he finished: 'A country with everyone like me would be ungovernable.'

Commenting on more EU directives for harmonization: 'You don't have to live under the same laws as a foreigner in order to trade with him. You don't have to take the same bath water.'

Just before Powell lost his Commons seat, he was walking

down a corridor in the Houses of Parliament and was greeted by the then Home Office minister, the Tory Sir Peter Lloyd, who commented how well Enoch looked. Powell scowled: 'Oh, it's come to that, has it?' Lloyd was baffled. 'What do you mean?' he asked. Enoch looked him in the eye: 'There are three ages of man – youth, middle-age and "Oh, you are looking well",' he snapped before disappearing down the corridor.

Bryan Gould was an extremely effective front-bench Labour spokesman and it was a big loss to his party when, before the advent of Blairism and New Labour, he decided to leave the House over differences with the then direction of his party.

Commenting on former National Heritage Secretary David Mellor, before the resignation of both men he said: 'He is in government principally because of his ability to give a good-news gloss to any disaster that turns up. He is a man who would have hailed the sinking of the *Titanic* as a first in underwater exploration. He would have greeted the Black Death as a necessary step towards a leaner and fitter economy. He would have celebrated the Great Fire of London as a vital contribution to urban regeneration.'

And on former Cabinet minister Michael Portillo: 'One of the most bizarre aspects has been the transformation of his personality on becoming a minister. When he began he was a man who was slightly austere, certainly rather detached and even commendably academic in style. Things changed when he changed his hairstyle to a sort of Heseltinian haystack. He then found that his eyes flashed, his lips curled, his nostrils flared and his voice vibrated with synthetic outrage. He gives all the appearance of having enrolled in a Youth Training Scheme leading to a diploma in the "Michael Heseltine School of Labour Bashing". Clearly, the qualifying test is the ability to spout absolute nonsense with utter conviction. The only point in which we can take comfort is that he shows no sign, so far, of reaching for the peroxide bottle.'

Lord Hailsham, the former Quintin Hogg, had an impressive career in politics, serving under five Prime Ministers until his retirement in 1987. Indeed, in the early 1960s he very nearly became Prime Minister himself but the Conservative hierarchy chose Sir Alec Douglas-Home instead. He would have made an interesting if unpredictable premier and might have prevented Harold Wilson securing a narrow Labour victory in 1964.

In his day he was a formidable orator. I remember being spellbound by his rhetoric when he came to Leicester in 1967 to speak at a by-election in support of the Tory candidate, Tom Boardman, who subsequently won what until then had been a safe Labour seat.

Hailsham was not only erudite but both colourful and emotional. One of the most effective and striking attacks (literally) that I have ever seen in a General Election campaign took place in 1966. Quintin Hogg, as he then was, was addressing an open-air rally for the Conservative Dudley Smith. During Hogg's speech, a Labour supporter, standing near the platform, raised a huge placard on which was pasted a poster showing the head and shoulders of Harold Wilson, with the slogan 'You Know Labour Government Works' printed underneath. Hogg immediately turned the incident to his own advantage by asking the crowd to look at the poster – 'the one with the ugly face'. He then launched a violent attack on the placard with his walking stick. The young Socialist was helpless. He was anchored to his place by the crowd and could not move. He was obliged to stand there, struggling to hold his poster and board upright, while a senior member of the Shadow Cabinet smashed it to smithereens! At least part of this incident was recorded by the television cameras and even today, over thirty years later, it is still an amusing, but effective, piece of political theatre.

Just as years later the media came to associate the phrase 'silly billy' with Labour's Denis Healey, Hogg's 1960s warning against Labour Party policy stuck, but not in the way he intended. During one interview he said: 'If the British public falls for the programme of the Labour Party, I say it will be stark raving bonkers.'

His view of fellow Tory Cabinet minister R. A. Butler, a fellow contender for the Tory leadership in the early 1960s: 'I never numbered candour amongst his virtues . . . he had not the stuff within him of which Prime Ministers are made. Politics may well include the art of the possible, but weakness on matters of principle, coupled with an inability to admit that you are wrong, limits the area of what is possible.'

On Socialism: 'It may be an excellent way of sharing misery, but it is not a way of creating abundance.'

On economists and their theories: 'The only thing I know about economic rules is that there are no economic rules.'

Even in the twilight of his ministerial career, his wicked sense of fun - and penchant for insults - had not deserted him. One day, during Hailsham's term as Lord Chancellor, the left-wing Bishop of Durham was making a rather polemical speech. A Labour peer who entered during this peroration was shocked to hear a loud voice bellow 'Bollocks!' at the bishop's remarks. Astonished he looked up, expecting to see a demonstrator being escorted from the public gallery above - but all was calm. He then realized that the insulting inter-ruption had come from the occupant of the Woolsack - Lord Hailsham.

Former Liberal MP, the heavyweight Cyril Smith, said of the British Parliament: 'The place is the longest running farce in the West End.'

And on the post-prandial activities of his political colleagues: 'The consumption of alcohol does tend to encourage those MPs of all parties who can neither speak with effect nor be silent with dignity.'

Norman (now Lord) Tebbit, former Tory Party Chairman, is a formidable parliamentary performer. Whatever the forum for debate, when Norman is on form you cross swords with him at your peril. He is undoubtedly, one of the most acid-tongued politicians of recent times.

When asked who had the most influence on him, his mother or his father, he replied: 'I don't think either of them had. I think I had more influence on them.'

When an MP sarcastically suggested to Norman that he was someone who no doubt held the view that 'God was a paid-up member of the Conservative Party,' Tebbit replied: 'Yes, of course he is. God could not be a Socialist because of the process of evolution.' When asked to explain what he meant, he said: 'Evolution means getting rid of the dinosaurs and replacing them with some more efficient and up-to-date animals. Any Socialist would have been dedicated to protecting the dinosaurs in the name of compassion or conservation or something. Thus dinosaurs would never have been allowed to go. So God can't be a Socialist.'

On the Labour Party: 'It is a party full of envy, people with failures and richly tainted with smug hypocrisy. It shows malice towards personal success.'

On politics: 'A centrally controlled state leads to unpleasant consequences. Socialism is bound to become authoritarian.'

When he was told that Labour Cabinet ministers in office were at least well-meaning, he exploded: 'Well-intentioned and well-meaning people are the most dangerous. You cannot have Socialism unless you control incomes and prices. So you go the way of Hitler and Mussolini.'

His view of those who attack the special relationship with America: 'Anti-American talk is a sign of cheap and dirty parties seeking cheap and dirty votes.'

Norman once astonished a group of MPs, of which I was one, when he suddenly broke off from talking about the economy to watch Labour MP David Winnick walk by. After watching in silence, he turned back and remarked: 'That man walks rather strangely. He has either got a bad tailor, suffers from piles or he's shit himself.'

On Labour's former leader: 'I have never rated Neil Kinnock as anything but a windbag whose incoherent speeches spring from an incoherent mind.'

And later, commenting further on Kinnock: 'More gimmicks than guts. I sometimes wonder whether he exists at all.'

On the Liberal Democrats: 'They are Enid Blyton Socialists – a dustbin for undecided votes.'

When Labour were at their nadir under Michael Foot, one Tory MP crowed with glee that 'The Labour Party are dead.' Tebbit corrected him: 'Not dead – just brain-dead.'

When he was told that he spent too much time trying to appease the party faithful, he shot back: 'The faithful won't vote for you unless you're faithful to them. I stand up for what I believe is right.'

On Tony Blair: 'He likes to style himself as the People's Prime Minister but the way the truth is concealed and distorted would do no credit to the former "People's" Republics of Eastern Europe. He appears to have no clear political views except that the world should be a nicer place and that he should be loved and trusted by everyone and questioned by no one.'

On New Labour MPs: 'Like glazed-eyed parrots, they all recite precisely the same words, transmitted by e-mail, fax or pager from Labour headquarters at Millbank. Labour MPs play no more part in Parliament than the Teletubbies.'

And, warming to this theme, his view on the House of Commons today: '"Blair's Babes" are shepherded through the division lobbies baa-ing like the well-fed sheep they are, without even sight of their great leader. He is too busy hosting parties for Labour luvvies and showbiz junkies at Number 10, or patronizing the nation with his views in a variety of silly voices on the selection of England's World Cup team. There is a whiff of arrogance and it is more than nannying.'

Once, while campaigning for Jeremy Hanley, also a future Tory Chairman, Norman was interrupted at a public meeting by an excitable young heckler. Tebbit tried to soothe the situation by saying: 'Calm down my lad,' it didn't seem to work and the young man retorted: 'My lad? You're not my father.' Tebbit silenced the barracking with the gibe: 'I would quit whilst you're ahead lad – I'm the only father you'll ever know.'

Former Labour leader Michael Foot has a forthright view of Norman Tebbit, calling him: 'A semi house-trained pole-cat.' Later asked to expand this view he added: 'He is the most stupendously offensive man in the House' – a description which Norman would probably regard as a compliment!

Foot's view of our National Anthem: 'The tune is appalling and the words are banal.' And when a minister remarked to him that he was 'too busy to read any books', Foot remarked: 'Men of power have no time to read; yet the men who do not read are unfit for power.' And Foot on John Major's government: 'Napoleon in his first 100 days recaptured Paris without a battle. John Major in his first 100 days buried Thatcherism without a tear. Thereafter, they were both destroyed for their previous misdeeds.'

The late Tory MP Dr John Blackburn was a likeable man who was very popular in the House. He would frequently greet colleagues with open arms and a cry of 'My son, my son' – even when the MP was old enough to be his father!

Despite several heart attacks, he insisted on attending at the Commons to vote whenever John Major's majority seemed at risk, even though the whips frequently told him to go home and rest. When I was Deputy Chief Whip I 'slipped' him from voting regularly, only to find he would reappear in votes hours later saying: 'I'm here to do my duty.' In the end, his loyalty killed him. He collapsed and died in the Commons precincts in October 1994 on the eve of the Tory Party Conference.

He rarely lost his temper and had a good sense of humour although he was not a great orator. On one occasion, during the 1979-83 Parliament, he sat all through a long debate on the subject of crime hoping to catch the Speaker's eye to deliver his speech, which he had spent several hours preparing. He was therefore both irritated and peeved when the debate ended without him having been called. Afterwards he approached the Speaker's chair to express his disappointment. 'Mr Speaker,' he began, 'I am very disappointed in you.'

'Why is that, John?' replied George Thomas, the Speaker.

'Well, Mr Speaker, you have denied the House the opportunity to hear a brilliant speech on this subject. I have in my pocket here a splendid speech and by not calling me you have denied the House the opportunity to hear this, the best speech I have *ever* prepared.'

'It's always the same with you John, isn't it?' Thomas retorted.

'What do you mean, Mr Speaker?' enquired Blackburn.

'Well, whenever I don't call you, you have prepared the most brilliant speech of all time, yet whenever I do call you, you always deliver a fucking awful one.'

To his credit, Blackburn not only took this well, he later told the story against himself.

In 1987 the members of an overseas British parliamentary delegation to Trinidad and Tobago were being bored by a particularly long-winded host, who insisted on relating details of a serious accident he had suffered many years earlier and of how he was subsequently ill for ages. After he had been going on for almost ten minutes about the one-time severity of his condition and how he had been at death's door, Dr Blackburn, the leader of the delegation, silenced him with the query, 'And tell me, did you live?'

TODAY'S BROADSIDES

The Father of the House of Commons, Sir Edward Heath, has been an MP since 1950. He has never been afraid to speak his mind – an attribute which has not endeared him to some of his parliamentary colleagues.

He was once offered a job by Lord Reith of the BBC. He turned it down with the barb: 'I couldn't work for God Almighty.'

He struck a chord with many when he commented on the high fees of directors of Lonhro PLC: 'The unpleasant and unacceptable face of capitalism.'

During a tour of the North-East area of England just before he became Prime Minister, he was taken through the slums of Newcastle. He surprised an aide when he remarked: 'If I lived here, I wouldn't vote for Harold Wilson.' He paused and added, 'I wouldn't vote for myself either – I'd vote for Robespierre.'

On the British press: 'A greater part of our press is run by foreigners; the Murdoch empire and the Black empire, and they have little interest in this country and its people. All they're interested in is their own products and making their own money.'

On Harold Wilson: 'A brilliant, if cynical party manager, who successfully got through his first period in office. But in the end, I ask, what did he really achieve? Or what did he really believe in?'

On his own party: 'The natural position of the Conservative Party is middle of the road. Always. Tony Blair realizes that, that is why he was so eager to seize this ground before the 1997 election. It remains to be seen how much of it he'll be able to keep.'

When one supporter criticized him for the fact that he was unmarried, he snapped back: 'What I do know is that a man who got married in order to be a better Prime Minister wouldn't be either a good Prime Minister or a good husband.'

Former Labour Cabinet minister, Denis (now Lord) Healey was a knockabout Commons performer who could be a bruiser in debate. In the 1980s he memorably insulted Margaret Thatcher saying: 'I often compare Mrs Thatcher with Florence Nightingale. She stalks through the wards of our hospitals as a lady with a lamp – unfortunately, in her case it is a blowlamp.' Later he added: 'Margaret Thatcher says that she has given the French President a piece of her mind – this is not a gift I would receive with alacrity.'

And on his own party's former leader, Harold Wilson: 'He did not have political principle. He had no sense of direction and rarely looked more than a few months ahead. He had short-term opportunism allied with a capacity for self-delusion, which made Walter Mitty appear unimaginative.'

His view of former American President Lyndon Johnson: 'He exuded a brutal lust for power which I found most disagreeable. He boasted acting on the principle "Give me a man's balls and his heart and mind will follow." He was a monster.'

Winston Churchill once remarked that Clement Attlee was 'a modest man with a lot to be modest about'. A Tory whip with a grudging respect for Healey quipped of him: 'Healey's a vain man – with a lot to be vain about.'

'She has the mouth of Marilyn Monroe and the eyes of Caligula' was President Mitterrand's verdict on Margaret Thatcher, Britain's first woman Prime Minister. Lady Thatcher is also one of Britain's longest-serving Prime Ministers. Elected Conservative Party leader in 1975, she led her party to victory in 1979, 1983 and 1987, before being deposed by her own MPs, following a challenge by Michael Heseltine. She later said of her challenger: 'He is all glamour and no substance.'

She was regarded by many political observers as an unknown quantity when she challenged Edward Heath for the Tory leadership after his second General Election defeat in 1974, having held only the relatively junior Cabinet position of Secretary of State for Education. There were also the patrician voices of the Conservative Party elders who thought that *no* woman could ever be up to the job of being PM. It was not long, however, before it was clear that she was not going to be a 'soft touch' for anyone.

One of the first pieces of invective aimed at her came from overseas, when the Russians called her 'The Iron Lady'. What was intended as an insult backfired badly as it was immediately used by her supporters as an indication of her steadfastness. The gibe has stuck but not in the way it was intended.

One apocryphal story going around the Tea Room at Westminster in the 1980s was that when Mrs T's receptionist answered the phone she used to say: 'I am afraid that Mrs Thatcher is not available at present. Who should I say was going to listen?'

Slapping down a colleague and summing up much of her own approach to politics, Mrs Thatcher said: 'Do you think you would ever have heard of Christianity if the Apostles had gone out and said: "I believe in consensus"?'

On the Labour government of Jim Callaghan: 'He presided over debt, drift and decay.'

On the sensitivities of most politicians: 'If you are working with politicians, you should remember that they have very large fingers and very large toes and you can tread on them remarkably easily. I, however, have stubs.'

In opposition, she silenced a Labour minister with: 'The honourable gentleman suffers from the fact that I understand him perfectly.'

She recently opined: 'One man's squabble is another man's discussion.'

And commenting on Prime Minister Tony Blair in 1999: 'Faced with a fight he's weak. He ought to be known as "Hands-up Blair." It is a pity we have not got a Prime Minister who will stand up for Britain. Blair leads the most feeble government this century – they are hollow and spineless.'

And Lady T, commenting on the pro-Euro Conservative MPs Ken Clarke and Michael Heseltine: 'I may be getting old but they are passé.'

She also observed: 'Being powerful is like being a lady. If you have to tell people you are, you aren't.'

Lord (Nigel) Lawson is one of those politicians who is respected more than liked. A serious heavyweight who has no time for political small-talk or the boring but sometimes necessary job of 'chatting-up' one's own backbenchers, particularly before a difficult debate. Indeed, on occasions, he actually appeared to enjoy *upsetting* his colleagues. One of these occasions was a PPS meeting held in the Lower Ministerial Conference Room, underneath the Commons Chamber.

This was a yearly occasion ahead of the Budget, to give PPSs the opportunity to let the Chancellor of the Exchequer know their views before he finalized his fiscal proposals. It was really little more than a public relations exercise. The job of being a PPS is generally a thankless one. These 'ministerial bag-carriers' work unpaid for ministers in the hope of one day attaining office themselves. This meeting was to give them the impression of being consulted before the Chancellor finalized his Budget plans, to make them perhaps think that their views *did* matter after all. Most knew it was something of a charade but they also knew their attendance would be expected and that the sessions would be chaired by the Chief Whip – the man who advises the Prime Minister of suitable candidates for promotion. This therefore presented an opportunity to show the Chief Whip who of those present was indeed promotion material. Most attending therefore asked questions and in past years the then Chancellor would respond politely and encouragingly. When Lawson was faced with this meeting, he did not hide his contempt. At the time, I was a PPS and consequently one of those in attendance. It was a memorable occasion.

'Nigel, you have started well,' a PPS pompously began, 'by abolishing a different tax in each Budget. But please Nigel, whilst continuing to maintain a sound economy, also continue with tax abolition and this year make it stamp duty.'

Lawson's features were impassive. 'You are right that I have abolished a tax in each Budget. If fiscal circumstances allow, this is something that I will continue to do. So far as stamp duty is concerned, when I first cut the level of this, the tax take went up because of increased taxable activity. Then, when circumstances allowed, I cut the stamp duty level again and much to the surprise of my officials the tax take did not go down but it went up, again because of increased dutiable activity. But, you know, if I abolish stamp duty completely, I think the tax take will go down. Next . . .!'

There was laughter all round and one PPS with a very red face. It was very amusing but after that episode, the questions dried up, the meeting finished early and this annual event was thereafter abandoned.

Although always on top of his brief, Lawson did not always bother with acquainting himself with the mundane background facts necessary for any minister undertaking a regional tour. In 1987, when touring seats in the East Midlands, Lawson came to speak for Tory candidate Andrew Mitchell, who was standing for Parliament for the first time in the Geddling constituency. The General Election was already underway and Lawson attended a public meeting on Mitchell's behalf. He astounded the audience – and Mitchell himself – by telling the crowd during his speech that they should '*re-elect* Andrew Mitchell' because he was 'doing such a good job in the House of Commons.' Mitchell, who went on to win, said afterwards that his constituents subsequently never believed another word uttered by a Cabinet minister.

Lawson's view on his colleague Jim (now Lord) Prior: 'An affable but short-fused Heathite squire.'

Long after he had left office, Lawson appeared on the Clive Anderson chat show on BBC TV to promote his book on dieting. Anderson, rather smugly, made a few quips at Lawson's expense. Not realizing perhaps that he was treading on thin ice, Anderson went on and on about Lawson's weight loss. Showing a flash of his old self, Lawson suddenly hit back saying: 'Well, it's better than having no neck!' Anderson appeared shocked at this swipe at his own physique, which was brutally effective. So effective in fact, that ever since I witnessed the episode, I have been totally unable to watch Anderson on television again. Each time he appears I find my eyes involuntarily drawn to where his neck should be!

Former Labour leader and now Euro Commissioner Neil Kinnock brought his party back towards the centre ground but failed to win as many had expected in 1992. He deserves credit for modernizing Labour but also the blame for Labour's 1992 loss. He was, simply, unelectable as Prime Minister and the sight of his ranting at Labour's Sheffield rally brought Tory voters out in their droves.

Always long-winded, he was sometimes worth listening to in the Commons. He once described former Conservative Party Chairman, Norman (now Lord) Tebbit as 'a boil on a verruca'.

And commenting on Tories Norman Fowler and Nigel Lawson, before Lawson undertook his spectacular diet: 'Norman Fowler looks as if he is suffering from a famine and Lawson looks as though he caused it.'

His view on former Labour minister David (now Lord) Owen: 'He possess an ego fat on arrogance and drunk on ambition.'

Labour minister Michael Meacher commenting on John Major's appointment of Peter Lilley as Secretary of State for Social Security: 'One likes to think that John Major has a sense of humour in some of his appointments. On this occasion I fear that the joke may be at the expense of the unemployed.'

Tory Michael Howard, the former Tory frontbencher, on Labour Chancellor Gordon Brown: 'He is a happiness Hoover. The gloom-monger in chief. When the story is grim, and the policies are dim, one knows that "it's got to be Gordon".'

On former Labour leader Neil Kinnock: 'As a pretender to the nation's driving seat, he has some notable qualifications. He loves reverse gear. His three-point turns are masterly.

And, as for his principles, he never sets out without a complete set of spares.'

Former Liberal leader Sir David (now Lord) Steel once silenced a heckler with the riposte: 'Of course I don't disagree with everything you say. Even a broken clock is right twice a day.'

Labour's Deputy Prime Minister John Prescott is a lively Commons performer although one always feels that a sudden loss of temper is bubbling just below the surface. It is probably for this reason that he acquired the nickname 'Thumper'.

Commenting on William Waldegrave being made Secretary of State for the Citizen's Charter: 'He has been described by John Major as the minister for little people – he seems more like the minister for paperclips to me.'

His view on the policy of privatization, when pursued by the Conservatives: 'It is to do with kick-backs, greed and sleaze in the Tory Party.'

Dismissing an attack from the Liberal Democrats, Prescott described them as: 'Always holier than holy.'

On the Conservatives' plans on rail privatization: 'This is not a Passenger's Charter. It is more a cherry-picker's charter – ripe for exploitation by property speculators, by route operators and by the Tories' City friends growing fat on commissions and fees resulting from the disposal of public assets.'

His view on outgoing Tory Chairman Lord Parkinson is terse: 'He's a nutter.'

Before 9 February 1998, not many Tory MPs had heard of the anarchist rock band Chumbawamba but now many admire group member Nigel Hunter (who uses the ridiculous stage name of Danbert Nobacon) for throwing a bucket of water over Prescott at the 1998 Brit Awards.

A back-bencher's view of the Deputy PM: 'he's a cross between Norman Tebbit, Andy Capp and Les Dawson.'

Former Deputy Prime Minister Michael Heseltine MP is a tremendous performer. Whether in the Commons, on the hustings or in a TV studio, when he is on form he can wipe the floor with anyone.

Commenting on Neil Kinnock: 'The self-appointed King of the Gutter.' He later added: 'He is a latter-day Duke of York leading a one-legged army: left, left, left . . .'

On Kinnock's successor John Smith: 'He is a fence-sitter. His policies are wall-to-wall whitewash.'

And, recently, effectively pointing out the difference between Old and New Labour: 'They used to be the barmy army. Now, they're the smarmy army'.

A few years ago he was speaking at a by-election meeting when a man in the audience wearing a large Labour rosette started protesting that the stewards were trying to make him remove his hat. He noisily resisted their attempts to make him sit down and remove his titfer. Heseltine silenced him with: 'I know why you don't want to take off your hat. It's because there's absolutely nothing underneath it.'

Michael Heseltine's views on Lady Thatcher are terse: 'A pugilistic little Englander.'

Rightly drawing attention to the fact that at the top of the Labour Party there are more Scots than Englishmen, he referred to Gordon Brown, Donald Dewar, Robin Cook, Brian Wilson, Dr John Reid and the others as 'Scotland's Revenge'.

Of his own career, he has said: 'I am humble enough to recognize that I have made mistakes, but politically astute enough to know that I have forgotten what they are.'

John Major was hailed as a refreshing change when he took over the reins of the Conservative Party from Margaret Thatcher in 1990. Towards the end of her term as Prime Minister, she was accused of being domineering, bossy, arrogant, out of touch and unwilling to consider the opinions of others. John Major was different. He listened. He consulted. He reflected on the concerns of others and was often cautious in his approach. This, plus a Labour leader whose temper always appeared to be hanging on a hair trigger, contributed to his surprise General Election win in 1992.

But public confidence in him did not last long. Disillusionment soon set in – even among some members of his own party – and his willingness to consult was soon portrayed by the press as indecision. He could be brilliant in a one-to-one interview in a TV studio. However, when he raised his voice, the rather thin timbre of his vocal chords, not noticeable when he was in conversation, did not carry well either in the Commons or on a public platform. But most of all it was his rapidly shrinking parliamentary majority which severely limited his room for manoeuvre. Major often took the blame for vacillation, when the real culprit was the parliamentary arithmetic.

Soon after his election as party leader, one Tory MP said of Major: 'I cannot stand his lowlier than thou attitude.'

Tony Blair, however, was extremely astute. Realizing Major's small parliamentary majority was limiting his options over a whole range of policy issues, he attacked the man himself, describing him as 'weak, weak, weak.' This theme was taken up by some sections of the press and was electorally damaging.

Occasionally, Major's own ministerial team were critical.

Former Tory Minister Nicholas Soames called his aims for a classless society 'a load of ullage'.

But Major often scored in a speech. Of New Labour he said: 'Unlike Labour, Conservatives aren't ashamed of our past. Unlike Labour, we haven't abandoned our principles and we haven't had to reinvent ourselves.'

Taking an effective swipe at Tony Blair's rhetoric: 'Have you noticed how the less a politician has to say, the more over-heated the language is? When every aim becomes a "crusade". Every hope a "dream". Every priority a "passion". Then it's time to duck for cover. When I hear Blair lace a speech with words like "tragedy", "triumph" and "destiny" – then I think of Ralph Waldo Emerson: "The louder he talked of his honour, the faster we counted our spoons." '

And again on Blair: 'He is sanctimonious and cloaks himself in righteousness.'

On proportional representation, he has forcefully argued the dangers of hung Parliaments: 'To offer the electorate a pro-portional Parliament that mirrors its opinions, but is unable to take decisions that mirror those opinions offers a false prospectus to the elector.'

On Labour's past: 'Labour often say they want to soak the rich. But they're the only party in history who regularly manage to soak the poor.'

And: 'Privately educated Tony Blair and privately educated Harriet Harman. You know what they say. New Labour, Old School Tie.'

After he had stepped down as Conservative leader and the country had experienced over a year of Labour government, he gave his views on Blair's style: 'He has "dumbed down" political debate to avoid scrutiny of Labour in office. It is all very well appearing on the *Des O'Connor Show* but it should not replace serious debate in Parliament. I cannot imagine Gladstone or Disraeli dumbing down politics like this.'

Commenting on Labour Home Secretary Jack Straw, he also revealed some of his own political tactics: 'Jack Straw has just made a speech in a very reasonable tone of voice. That makes me suspicious. When I was a minister and I was excessively reasonable, it usually meant that I had something to hide, or that I sided with the Opposition, but did not wish my own party to realize this.'

BBC interviewer John Humphreys recently claimed to be still baffled by Major's response during the Tory leadership election when Major resigned to seek his own re-election. According to Humphreys, when he asked Major why he had taken this extraordinary step, he received the reply: 'When your back's against the wall, the only thing to do is turn around and fight.'

To some observers, Major however, failed the Harold Wilson test of the qualities required of a Prime Minister. Wilson's theory was that 'No one should attempt the role of PM who cannot fall asleep the moment he is in bed with the cares and worries of the day behind him.'

Whatever else he achieves, history will credit Tony Blair with helping to bring to an end eighteen years of Conservative government – the longest period of one-party rule since the Crimean War. And he did it by a far bigger margin than anyone expected, winning the largest parliamentary majority for any party since 1832.

Only a few years on from this historic victory and many have already forgotten that, when he was first elected as Labour leader, the Prime Minister acquired the nickname of 'Bambi', so unsure was his touch. However, as he found his feet, this soubriquet soon disappeared.

Indeed, it did not take long for MPs to notice that his confidence had grown so much in such a short space of time, he soon seemed to have an absolute faith in himself, which to some Tories appeared to be dangerously close to hubris.

However, there is no doubting the charm that this public school barrister can exude, although critics would say his apparent artless sincerity can sometimes look rehearsed and calculated. It is far too early to judge his achievements but his current control over both his ministers and his party, and the effectiveness of his spin doctors, are extremely impressive and so far few Labour MPs have dared to question the style or direction of their leader.

Blair's method is markedly different from John Major. He has imposed a rigid and centralized control of the government machine from Downing Street. However, one Labour left-winger prefers to use the soubriquet 'Phoney Blur' in view of Blair's large-scale dumping of his party's left-wing policies and principles.

Recently, dismissing an attack on Labour's foreign policy towards Sierra Leone, Blair described it as 'an overblown hoo-hah'.

On the official Opposition: 'The policy of the Conservative Party was a mess before the election and has been a catastrophe since. If there is any brain left in the Opposition it is time that they manifested it.'

On being attacked by the Tories on Europe: 'The one issue that I would have thought it very unwise to raise is the subject of Europe, where the Conservative Party is split from head to toe.'

On John Major: 'He presided over the most wasteful,

inefficient and incompetent government in living memory. His hope before the 1997 election was that the public forget VAT on fuel, Black Wednesday, BSE, the doubling of crime, the doubling of debt, the poll tax, arms for Iraq, cash for questions, Scott, Nolan, business failures and negative equity. Major pretends he has no responsibility for the state of the nation he has governed. It's as if he had just landed from Mars.'

Blair's swipe at Tory MP John Bercow: 'His hallmark is to be both nasty and ineffectual in equal quantities.'

On William Hague: 'He requires lessons in how to be leader of the Opposition. If he is really good to me, I might tell him. He gets up and asks what might impress a sixth-form debating society but does not impress me.'

And again on Hague: 'Quite the most bizarre experience is to be preceded by the leader of the Opposition running around the country, holding press conferences and saying what a disaster everything is. The fact is that no one pays the slightest attention to him but that is more a reflection on him than anything else.'

Blair on the Conservatives' economic philosophy: 'These are people who believe that a strong economy can be built on sweatshop wages. They believe that the answer to the problems of the economy is low wages.'

Returning to his attack on the Tories: 'William Hague and his party have still not worked out why they lost the last election. He ought to try to work out where the Conservatives stand on some of the policy issues that face us.'

On the Conservative Shadow DTI Spokesman John Redwood: 'Recently Redwood complained that former German Chancellor Helmut Kohl should not have been given the freedom of the City of London. Perhaps it is now time that William

Hague gave *him* the freedom of the Conservative back benches.'

Former Euro Commissioner Leon Brittan's views on Tony Blair's style of government: 'It's government by spinning.'

A Tory Whip on Tony Blair: 'Tony is a real politician. He can say absolutely nothing and mean it.'

While recently a Labour left-winger was overheard describing the Prime Minister as: 'Phoney Toe-Knee.'

In 1997, expressing his own frustration at leading a party which had been in Opposition for so long, Blair said that he 'had a PhD in Opposition'. Only time will tell whether he earns one in government.

Commenting on William Hague in 1999: 'On Europe his policy is decided by those he has surrounded himself with – lunatics and headbangers.'

Disputes between the Houses of Lords and Commons have usually been decided by compromise. However, in 1998, when the Lords threw out Tony Blair's electoral proposals for Europe, he not only decided to use the Parliament Act to override the Upper House, but decided to proceed with proposals to change the composition of the Lords itself, without all-party agreement. This led one MP to sing a new version of *Rule Britannia: Rule Britannia, Britannia waves the rules!*

Although they are regularly accused of being voting fodder, not all of Tony Blair's back-benchers have kept their heads down. Veteran Labour MP Austin Mitchell recently described New Labour as: 'A children's crusade which regards older MPs as useless and yet the young make the biggest messes.' He went on to blame Gordon Brown for 'locking the government into deflation' and Peter Mandelson for 'the Dome disaster', while calling former minister Harriet Harman 'the Minister for Social Insecurity'. He added: 'Boy wonders run Labour and to be old is a bit of an inconvenience.'

Former Labour MP Reginald Paget's gibe at Harold Wilson's government in 1964 would probably be applied by some present-day Labour MPs to Tony Blair's administration. Paget said: 'I did not come here to substitute for an upper-middle class Conservative government a lower-middle class conservative one.'

Tory leader William Hague is still largely underrated outside Westminster. This is likely to change as he has still not yet had sufficient time to fully make his mark on public opinion. What he has shown however, since he was elected Opposition leader in 1997, is that he is an extremely effective Commons performer.

After his election as Tory leader, many commented on Hague's Yorkshire accent and his somewhat nasal delivery. Arthur Worlsey, the ventriloquist observed: 'He sounds like someone trying to impersonate Mike Yarwood impersonating Harold Wilson.'

As might be expected, Hague has been extremely critical of Blair's style of government. Taking a swipe at New Labour he said: 'This is the government of the nanny state. This is the government who tell people how to live. They tell people: "don't drink, don't smoke, don't hunt, don't have a pension, don't eat beef on the bone, don't save, don't drive a car; if you drive a car don't park it." Tony Blair preaches to us and Labour's Budgets represent the collection plate being passed round after the service.'

After news of Cherie Blair's £2,000 hairdressing costs for a USA trip were made public, Hague quipped: 'The most expensive haircut I ever had cost a tenner. And £9 went on the search fee."

Commenting on the Prime Minister's attitude to the Mother

of Parliaments, Hague said: 'Blair wants a rubber-stamp Parliament where MPs only turn up to fawn over him.'

On the difference between the Prime Minister and former Labour Agriculture Minister and now Labour's 'Cabinet enforcer' Jack Cunningham, Hague quipped: 'Tony Blair gave up the Bar for politics. Jack Cunningham appears to sometimes give up politics for the bar.'

On Deputy Prime Minister John Prescott's transport plans: 'After all the promises and all the hype, it is now clear that it is a complete dog's breakfast.'

Hague on former Paymaster General Geoffrey Robinson, who was widely criticized for his off-shore tax trusts: 'Blair appointed as the minister responsible for offshore tax avoidance a man with offshore tax trusts. This is breathtaking hypocrisy. I suspect that the Swiss bank family Robinson will stay in business and out of tax.'

Following his absence in 1998 during a short illness, Hague bounced back with a vicious swipe at the New Labour government in the wake of revelations that one lobbyist appeared to suggest ministers were available upon payment of a fee. Hague commented: 'even with my sinuses, I could smell the stench coming out of these [lobbying] revelations. This is a government for sale.' Continuing, he challenged Blair: 'When are you going to stop protecting the money-grabbing cronies you've surrounded yourself with?' And for good effect he added: 'they are feather-bedding, pocket-lining, money-grabbing cronies.'

Returning to the charge, Hague later said that the Blair government had: 'Too many cronies and not enough principles.'

On Labour: 'The British Labour Party is an organization where your best friend will plunge a knife in your back and then call the police to tell them that you are carrying a concealed weapon.'

Commenting on Blair's first year as PM: 'In just one year, a man with confident early pledges has become full of meaningless waffle.'

During 1998, dogged by domestic scandals, but still in office, Bill Clinton earned the sobriquet, 'The Comeback Kid.' When Peter Mandelson, Blair's right-hand man, was forced to resign because of his whopping, undisclosed loan from Geoffrey Robinson, Hague effectively remarked on the difference between the two men: 'Peter Mandelson is not the Comeback Kid – he the Kickback Kid.'

On Foreign Secretary Robin Cook: 'The Foreign Office is being run like a Dad's Army outfit by a Foreign Secretary who combines the pompousness of Captain Mainwaring, the incompetence of Private Pyke and the calm of Corporal Jones.'

In the opinion of many Tories, Hague has made an excellent start in modernizing the Conservative Party. Not so MP Nicholas Winterton, however. Commenting on Hague's plans, the Tory MP was succinct: 'They're Stalinist.'

Former Conservative Party Chairman Lord Parkinson taking a swipe at the Labour government quipped: 'The trouble with New Labour MPs is that most of them don't trust each other – and they're right.'

And, early in 1998, poking fun at his own political comeback as Party Chairman he said: 'I have at least proved one thing – you can boil a cabbage twice.'

Former DTI Minister Peter Mandelson is known as either 'The Prince of Darkness' or 'The King of Spin' depending on what your politics are. Within hours of Labour's election victory, when he was neither a Cabinet minister nor a departmental one, he issued instructions to government departments to clear future policy announcements through the Prime Minister's Office. He explained his action by saying: 'It is important to have a strong centre of government. Civil servants can sometimes be rather tunnel-visioned.' Rather immodestly, he has referred to himself as 'The Quality Controller.'

Even as a backbencher, he certainly wields huge power, and is an expert at what some regard as the main evil of politics in the 90s.

In 1998, taking a swipe at former Home Secretary Michael Howard, who had criticized Foreign Secretary Robin Cook for sacking his diary secretary Anne Bullen, he said: 'Michael Howard has traded the responsibilities of high office for breathless interviews about a diary secretary. The man who sacked the Director General of the Prison Service to cover his back and was successfully sued for damages has taken to his high horse on personnel matters.'

Of the Tories generally he said: 'By addressing only the diary column end of politics, the Conservatives are reinforcing the public's opinion of them as out of touch and irrelevant to the issues of today. By concentrating their firepower on dishwashers and diary secretaries the Tories devalue their attacks and emphasize why they were so distrusted by the electorate.'

He then went on to describe the official Opposition under William Hague as: 'Pathetic and frivolous.'

Such is Mandelson's perceived power over New Labour MPs, that some Conservatives have taken to telling a story of a newly elected New Labour MP who went for a haircut wearing earphones connected to a Walkman tape recorder. The MP refuses to remove his headset and insists that the barber work around it. While sitting in the chair the MP falls asleep, so to make his job easier, the hairdresser removes the earphones. After a couple of minutes, the MP slumps forward – dead. Shocked, the barber picks up the headset to hear what it was the MP was listening to, and he hears the voice of Peter Mandelson saying: 'Breathe in . . . Breathe out . . . Breathe in . . . Breathe out . . .'

One story currently going around Westminster is that a number of Labour MPs have been phoning the Department of Trade and Industry and asking to speak to 'the Secretary of State, Peter Mandelson.' When the receptionist replies: 'Peter Mandelson resigned months ago,' the response from the Labour MPs is always the same: 'I know he resigned ages ago, but I just wanted to hear someone say it again.'

Comment by a Labour MP in the Commons Tea Room: 'Peter reminds me of a character from a horror film. He's Dr Mandelstein.'

Not many outside the world of politics understand the purpose of parliamentary Whips although they do realize that whipping is something of a black art. Most perceive that whipping involves the arm-twisting of our MPs or councillors.

Party Whips, or 'Whippers in' as they were once known – the name comes from fox-hunting parlance and not some sadistic ritual – originated in the early eighteenth century. At Westminster, all parties have whips. They are MPs whose job it is to secure the maximum possible attendance of their own party colleagues, in the right voting lobby, during a vote.

Understandably, the press usually focus on this: the Whips' ability – or sometimes inability – to secure votes for their own party on difficult issues. But, although this is the prime duty of any Whips' office, there is more to whipping than just that. In one way, a good Whips' office is like a sewer. The work is mainly underground, is largely unseen and may not be very pleasant but it is essential to the workings of both Houses.

Although the Whips' main duty is one of management and persuasion, they also act as a conduit for the passage of information. They will note the emerging views of party colleagues. For example, mounting dissent from Labour MPs about the way their government is handling an issue will be conveyed by government Whips to the Chief Whip who in turn will notify the Prime Minister. This then may lead to a change of presentation, or a change of policy or, where a government with a small majority fails to take heed, defeat on the floor of the House. This is, of course, a highly unlikely eventuality at present, given Tony Blair's rather obscene majority, which some say has allowed him to treat the present House of Commons with contempt.

Party Whips have various methods of persuading colleagues not only to wait for a late vote but also to support their own side when the vote comes. A number of years ago it used to be the practice of the Conservative Party to station a Whip at each exit of the Palace of Westminster during the early part of the evening. This custom was known as 'all doors'. The Whips would then stop all of their own party's MPs as they were leaving, telling them to remain until all votes had been concluded.

This system had one serious flaw. The Whips had to be able to immediately recognize all members of their own party – no mean feat just after a General Election. On one occasion during 'all doors', Walter Bromley-Davenport MP, a new junior government Whip, was trying to prevent Conservative MPs from leaving before the business had finished. He approached a familiar-looking young man whom he took to be a new Tory MP. 'Where are you going?' he snapped.
'I'm going home,' came the reply.
'No you're not, you're staying for the next vote,' Bromley-Davenport retorted.

'Why should I stay for the next vote?' the obstinate young man replied. At this Bromley-Davenport lost his temper. 'You are staying here!' he shouted and kicked the young man in the seat of his pants. He was mortified to discover shortly afterwards that he had been addressing the Belgian Ambassador. His career in the Whips' office ended the next day.

Today, new technology has come to the rescue. Whips now notify their party colleagues of voting via an electronic pager.

The faux pas of Mr Bromley-Davenport could never happen to Sir Sydney Chapman MP, who is far too courteous and polite. Indeed, Sir Sydney is one of the most gracious MPs in the House. During the 1987-92 Parliament, when Sir Sydney was serving as a senior Whip, he once had to telephone a number of backbenchers to ask them to return for an unexpected late vote. Upon telephoning then Tory MP Andrew Mitchell, he was informed by a French-sounding female voice at the other end of the phone that the MP was not at home but was expected shortly. Sir Sydney explained who he was and said that he wanted to speak to the MP urgently and could be contacted in the Whips' office. Mr Mitchell never telephoned back, nor did he appear at the vote, despite Sir Sydney's very clear instruction.

On seeing Mr Mitchell in the House the next day, Sir Sydney inquired why he had not returned the call and why he had not voted. 'Oh, was it you?' the MP said. 'When I got home the au pair said that she had a phone call from a very strange man and that when he started to talk about whipping, she just put down the phone.'

Over the years, Sir Sydney Chapman has had to suffer more than his fair share of long boring speeches from visiting politicians. He has a unique way of dealing with the problem. Whenever he is asked to say Grace, he recites:

> 'Oh Lord please bless this food and wine,
> And those here present about to dine,

But if long speeches we must endure,
Pray God they serve a good liqueur.'

A politician faced with a lively rugby club audience, may, however, prefer the Grace once told to me by world-famous ventriloquist Arthur Worsley:

'Thank you Lord for everything,
The food, the wine and all,
Thank you for all the creatures,
be they great or small.
And if I should return to earth,
within this self-same figure,
Please Lord, leave me as I am,
but with my penis six inches bigger.'

The government Whips' office is the only department in government where the incumbents choose who is to be newly promoted to their number. In all other departments the choice is that of the Prime Minister, although the PM does have a veto over the Whips' choice if he feels the person is unsuitable. The Whips make their choice by a 'blackball' system, whereby any one Whip can object to a person being admitted to the office.

Sir Sydney Chapman is a former Vice-Chamberlain of Her Majesty's Household, and as I have mentioned, in the last Parliament he was a senior member of the Tory government Whips' office. He therefore knows the system well. He frequently tells the story, which may be apocryphal, of a particular MP who was rather over-ambitious and pushy. A rumour circulated that the said MP was about to be invited to join the Whips' office. To his colleagues' amazement the MP breezed in to the Commons Smoking Room and started to order champagne all round. As each Whip entered, the MP would bellow out: 'Ah, here comes my *friend*.' He was therefore extremely disappointed when the official announcement the next day revealed that someone else had got the position.

Taking the unprecedented step of trying to find out what had gone wrong, he approached one of the Whips and said: 'I had heard that I was to be the new Whip. Presumably I was blackballed because one of the Whips didn't like me. Tell me, who was it?' He was silenced with the reply: 'Well, I can't actually say how many blackballed you – but have you ever seen sheep shit?'

Before the 1997 election, when the Conservatives were over 20 points behind in the opinion polls, Mr Chapman was asked at a meeting to describe his position in British politics. He replied: 'A politician is someone who thinks only of the next election but a statesman is someone who thinks beyond that to the next generation. Ladies and gentlemen, standing before you, you see a statesman. In view of my party's standing in the polls at the present time, I just dare not *think* of the next election.'

Before the 1992 General Election, a Northern Ireland Office PPS (the lowest form of government life) was giving his views on the tactics of the IRA to a number of Tory MPs in the Member's Tea Room. He gave an extremely long and boring explanation of why IRA bombers behaved in a particular way and was totally oblivious to the fact that his colleagues had long since tired of his tedious and pompous exegesis. Rambling on, he referred to a recent terrorist attack and claimed that his theory showed that the bombers had actually hit the wrong target, adding: 'The IRA actually meant to bomb M&S but instead they hit B&Q.' Mr Chapman, who as I have revealed, is normally the epitome of civility, could stand it no longer. Interjecting, he ended the discussion with the barb: 'Perhaps the bombers were dyslexic.'

A fellow Tory Whip commenting recently on Sir Sydney: 'He must be an optimist. Even his suit has its shiny side.'

Former Chief Whip Richard Ryder (now Lord Ryder of Wensum) hit the mark when he said of those MPs who insist on speaking in the Commons at a late hour: 'MPs who speak after ten o'clock at night do not win arguments, they just lose friends.'

Seeing his junior Whip David Davis MP at a wedding, Ryder remarked: 'What are you doing here – you're the funeral Whip.'

Former Tory Chief Whip and Foreign Office Minister Sir Alistair Goodlad MP likes to tell the story of a Russian dissident who is questioned on suspicion of subversion by the KGB (who, in their methods, are I suppose roughly akin to the Whips' office). They raid his house and confiscate all of his property which is taken away for examination, including his pet parrot. He is arrested and asked if he wants to say anything which could be used in evidence at his trial. 'Yes,' the dissident replies, 'I just want you to know that I don't agree with the political views of the parrot.'

A few years ago, a new Conservative MP, upon hearing that a colleague had been accused of corruption, approached his then Chief Whip to ask how he could be sure, when accepting a gift, that he was not breaking the House of Commons' rules. He was stunned by the reply: 'The guidelines are simple,' he was told by the Chief Whip. 'If you can eat it, drink it or fuck it, it's not bribery.'

Former Tory Deputy Chief Whip and Industry Minister Greg Knight, commenting on New Labour's decision to keep its candidates 'on message' during the 1997 election: 'During this election, all Labour candidates have a speech impediment . . . Peter Mandelson.'

During the last Parliament, when John Prescott was Labour's Transport spokesman, Mr Knight was, for the most part, a government Whip. During one particular debate, Prescott was outlining what changes he would like to see in the transport field and suggested that British law should be changed to allow random breath-testing of motorists. Knight, sitting on the government front bench, muttered 'What rubbish' at this suggestion and Prescott exploded. He abandoned his speech and accused Conservatives of not taking the issue of random breath tests seriously. 'The only thing they really take seriously is bringing back the death penalty,' Prescott bellowed. Then, pointing at Knight, he added: 'I bet he supports hanging.'
Knight shot back: 'Yes, but not random hanging.'

On the announcement of Labour's election victory, he quipped: 'Fool Britannia.'

On Frank Dobson: 'Forgotten but not gone.'

On Tony Blair: 'He's so vain he'd take his own hand in marriage.'

Sometimes MPs can be discomfited by colleagues unintentionally. In 1992, Knight's neighbouring parliamentary seat of Erewash was won by fellow Tory Angela Knight, who is no relation. However, on returning to the Commons, Greg Knight was approached by two Labour MPs who stopped to congratulate him on the fact that 'his wife' had joined him in the Commons. 'But we are not married,' Knight protested. One of the Labour MPs looked shocked: 'Well, it's about time you made an honest woman of her then,' he bellowed before disappearing down the corridor.

In 1987, and at a time when he sported a beard, Knight was

interrupted at a public meeting in Derby by a man who shouted out: 'Aren't all politicians liars?'

Stroking his beard, he retorted: 'Well, at least you can't call me a bare-faced one.'

One evening when Knight was dining in the Members' Dining Room with a couple of MPs, the affable and ebullient fellow Tory Nicholas Soames joined his table. Soames had hardly sat down, when he jabbed a fork into one of his colleagues' meals and bellowed: 'Is that tripe?'

Knight enquired: 'To which end of the fork are you referring?'

On being newly elected to the Commons, when he was asked by a local journalist what his Commons office was like, he replied: 'It's so small I have to go outside to change my mind.'

Between 1983 and 1997, he served as a government minister and during that time had responsibility in one form or another for most of the departments of state. Asked about his experience in politics by a group of students, he replied: 'Having held office under two Prime Ministers and four Chief Whips, I have formed the view that life in politics is very much like being in a dog-sled team. Unless you are the lead dog, the view doesn't really change much.'

On political pay: 'Times have changed. One thing that John Major did which has greatly improved the quality of life for MPs and ministers is something for which he will never receive public credit. He gave politicians a substantial pay rise. When Labour ministers reflect on their current financial position, they should remember that when I was first made a minister I was so underpaid I used to cash my salary cheque on the bus. And when I was a junior Whip and decided to buy a hi-fi, I had to ask the store for three days to pay – Christmas, Easter and Whit.'

To one businessman who at a dinner remarked loudly that he had 'no time for politics or politicians', Knight replied with the words of Plato: 'Those who are too smart to engage in politics are punished by being governed by those who are dumber.'

At a reception during a conference, Knight found himself sitting near to a red-headed woman who was drinking heavily. After a few moments she started raising her voice to another woman sitting next to her. Trying to calm the situation, Knight said: 'It is apparently true what they say about red-heads and their temper.' The woman immediately tried to stand up and it became clear that she was drunk. 'Well, smart Alec,' she replied, 'you are quite wrong because my hair colour comes from a bottle!'
Knight retorted: 'Clearly, madam, so does your temper!'

On Ian Paisley MP: 'Just occasionally I wish he would use words of one decibel.'

Commenting on former Labour Deputy Leader Roy Hattersley: 'A man who has made a meteoric disappearance.'

On former Tory Whip Tim Wood, who used to work in computers before entering politics: 'He knows all there is to know about the state of the Ark computers and trailing-edge technology.'

On former Tory premier Sir Edward Heath: 'The Incredible Sulk.'

And, in the 1992-97 Parliament, commenting on Labour MP Dr Jeremy Bray: 'He is living proof that there is life after death.'

On fellow Tory Eric Forth MP: 'I won't say his sideburns are long, but when I first met him I thought he was on the phone.'

On *New Labour's* Policy Review: 'More somersaults than Billy Smart's Circus.'

On Euro Commissioner Neil Kinnock, when he was Labour Party Leader, in 1991, he was vicious: 'He has the temperament of John McInroe and the intelligence of Eddie the Eagle. He will never be British Prime Minister. What Britain needs is a consolidator, not a contortionist; a winner not a windbag; a victor not a vasectomy.'

And, on the policy of the Whips Office in which he served: 'In defeat, malice, in victory, revenge.'

On fellow Tory, Phillip Oppenheim: 'His policy towards women appears to be that a bird in the hand is worth two in the phone book.'

And, commenting again on former Tory Whip, the computer-loving Tim Wood: 'He has almost become at one with his computer. I suppose he has reached Nerdvana.'

In the mid 80s, Knight was persuaded, against his better judgement, to speak at a Rugby Club dinner. He was told beforehand by the organizer that they wanted a fairly serious speech. However, by the time the audience sat down for the meal, most of the crowd were inebriated and the air was filled with bread rolls being thrown from one table to the other. After the chairman's slurred introduction Knight rose, told a few jokes and then, before heading for the door, he recited:

> 'A man may kiss a maid goodbye,
>   The sun may kiss a butterfly,
> The morning dew may kiss the grass,
>   And you my friends . . . farewell.'

The late Conservative MP Sir David Lightbown was extremely taciturn most of the time and this was just one of the reasons why he was an excellent whip. However, he never refrained from speaking his mind if he felt that a parliamentary colleague was being disloyal and, unlike Sir Sydney

Chapman, he was quite prepared to be disagreeable if he felt that the miscreant deserved to feel the lash of his tongue.

This could be a terrifying experience. Lightbown, a former footballer, was physically a huge man and his very presence could be intimidating to young backbench MPs – and he knew it.

He always smiled wryly when the press referred to his weight because they invariably described him as 'the Commons most-feared whip, who weighs 18 stone'. This was a considerable *understatement* of his size, so he was flattered rather than insulted. For a time we both served as household officers – senior government whips whose duty it is to attend upon the monarch on ceremonial occasions.

During the State Opening of Parliament in 1994, David and I were both obliged to attend at Buckingham Palace to 'escort' the Queen to the Palace of Westminster. In effect, all we had to do was ride together in the Queen's procession to Parliament, in one of the horse-drawn coaches of state with two other palace officials.

Now these coaches look huge from outside but looks are deceptive. The coaches are tall, certainly, but with four people aboard, they are extremely cramped inside. Also their 'suspension' is extremely primitive and amounts to no more than a huge spring for each wheel, rather like an early child's pram. As a consequence, the coaches bounce around quite a lot, rather like a vehicle without shock absorbers. As David struggled to climb in, his weight made the coach lurch violently over to the side, causing one of the footmen to mutter, not so *sotto voce*: 'Blimey, I think we'd better put an extra horse on.'

He was furious when former Chancellor of the Exchequer Norman Lamont starting rocking the political boat after he was sacked by John Major. Asked by a journalist what he thought of Mr Lamont's resignation speech he said: 'As far as

I'm concerned he can go and play his fiddle in the fields on his own – and die in the grass.'

On former Scottish Office Minister Hector Munro he was more sympathetic: 'It's amazing. All the years he's been in the House and he still hasn't got an idea. He spent twenty minutes talking garbage about some obscure thing in the Highlands.'

Lightbown was never a fan of Michael Heseltine but acknowledged his qualities, remarking after the political row over Heseltine's plans to close a number of coal mines: 'You've got to hand it to him. He's the only politician who can dig himself into a hole AND out again within a week.'

Once, in the Commons Tea Room, a new MP was bragging about his former occupation: 'I used to be a plant manager,' he boasted. Lightbown was unimpressed. 'I bet it was his job to water them,' he muttered as he left.

He was always loyal to those he served but was never one to mince his words. Despite all whips being instructed to keep quiet in public, he went on television during the 1992 Conservative Party Conference to call the Tories Maastricht rebel MPs 'nutters'.

He once described one Euro-sceptic Welsh MP as a man who was: 'So thick, he wouldn't make an adequate parish councillor even in a bad year.'

On one occasion, seeing John Prescott enter the House of Commons Tea room, Lightbown shouted: 'Make yourself at home John – hit somebody.'

He once petrified a young provincial journalist who criticized the Whips' office by giving him a menacing stare, and saying: 'Listen, sonny, one of my ancestors helped kill King Edward the Second by ramming a red-hot poker up his arse. If you don't watch out the process will be repeated.'

In 1990, when attending the Conservative Party Conference,

I was invited to a dinner organized by a regional television company. I sat next to one of the company directors who seemed rather apprehensive and nervous and he kept looking warily in my direction. After the meal was over, he relaxed and admitted that he had been jittery because I was 'only the second Whip' he had met. He continued: 'The first time we asked a whip to this dinner it was David Lightbown and when I made some constructive criticism of the policies being pursued by Mrs Thatcher, he suddenly stood up and said: "Have you ever been head-butted, sonny?"'

Lightbown once asked a newly elected Tory MP: 'Why are all the windows sealed at Liberal headquarters?' The new member did not know. Lightbown quipped: 'To keep all the fairies from flying out.'

At one of Lightbown's advice surgeries in his Staffordshire seat, a constituent came to see him about the inadequacies of the Child Support Agency. The woman, clearly upset, felt that too much money was being taken away from her husband to support his children by an earlier liaison. 'We've got no money,' she complained, adding: 'I just feel like committing suicide.' The woman then pointed to the first-floor window of Lightbown's office: 'In fact I am so depressed, I could just jump out of that window over there,' she cried. Lightbown stood up. 'Look dear, if you want to jump out of a window and commit suicide that's fine by me but you don't do it here. Go home – and then you can jump out of your own window.'

But it would be wrong to think of Lightbown just as a menacing bully, a view which some of these episodes might encourage. If he thought he was being taken advantage of, or if a colleague had been disloyal to his own party, he was fearsome. But when faced with a genuine human tragedy, David Lightbown was always the first to offer his support. He was a great character and politics is so much the poorer for his passing.

Opposition Deputy Chief Whip Patrick McLoughlin on a party colleague: 'He's so full of himself he never gets lonely.'

And on Labour's Dennis Skinner: 'He reminds me of Boxer in *Animal Farm*. Even if his party's tune changes dramatically, he can always be relied on to change his tune accordingly. "Stick with it all the way, it's sure to get better" appears to be his motto.

The all-powerful Chairman of the Public Accounts Committee of the House of Commons is David Davis MP, a former Tory whip and Foreign Office Minister. When asked his view on a colleague, he replied: 'he is about as much use as the Pope's testicles.'

Once, during Foreign Office questions, when Robin Cook was still in Opposition and Davis was at the Dispatch Box facing Cook, Labour's Barry Sheerman shouted out: 'Two-faced Tories.' Davis immediately turned the insult back on Labour. Looking at Cook, he replied: 'Well, no one would accuse Robin Cook of being two-faced. If he was, he wouldn't wear that one.'

Before the collapse of the USSR, Opposition Whip John M. Taylor MP had occasion to visit the Berlin Wall. He was amazed at the extent of the graffiti daubed on this symbol of Eastern bloc repression. He found himself scanning the scrawl to find something written in English, when his eyes lit upon the words 'Geoff Boycott – we love you.' He continued his trip and then returned to Britain where the following evening he was the guest speaker at a function organized by his local cricket club.

During the course of giving his views on world events he mentioned the very moving experience he had had visiting the Berlin Wall and added how he had searched the graffiti for some message written in English. He explained to them how the first intelligible sentence he had seen was 'Geoff Boycott – we love you'. On hearing this, some wag at the back of the room shouted out: 'Which side of the wall was it written on?' It was at that point he felt he started to lose his audience.

Former Tory Whip Robert Hughes silenced Labour back-bencher Eric Martlew with the barb: 'He reminds me of one of those shredded wheat advertisements. He speaks bravely and beats his chest saying that he wants to debate an issue, but when it was suggested that the House might sit late, he starts whingeing.'

No Whip or ex-Whip from any party has yet revealed all that goes on in the Whips' office, although, to his shame, former Tory MP Gyles Brandreth has got close to so doing. He was wrong to break the Whips code of silence. Having been frequently approached by the press for the inside story on how Whips work, I am strongly of the opinion that 'Whipping, like stripping, is best done is private.'

Gyles Brandreth commenting recently on Labour's Deputy Leader John Prescott: 'He is plug-ugly, overweight and overbearing.'

Lord Cecil Parkinson on the working of the Whip's office: 'The Whips like to give you what they think you deserve, and deny you what they think you want.'

Foreign Secretary Robin Cook on the official Opposition: 'Conservatives cannot get off the back foot because that foot is so mired in the mud of the last Tory government.'

Former National Heritage Secretary David Mellor was a formidable Commons performer and his defeat at the 1997 General Election was a big loss to the Conservative parliamentary team.

Respected more than liked, his hard-working, intelligent and pugnacious style is not so much hard-hitting as brutal. He received loud cheers from both the Tory and Labour benches when he said of the Liberal Democrats in the Commons: 'None of their MPs are household names – not even in their own home.'

In the late 1980s, Mrs Thatcher's proposed health reforms were being attacked from all sides, usually from positions of ignorance. The Labour Party shamelessly exploited genuine concern about the planned changes and threw their full weight into heightening public disquiet. I make no complaint about this but others, who should have known better, added to the unease and uncertainty by making wild and unsubstantiated claims that the poor and vulnerable would not get proper health care. Public concern reached such a level that even the usually unflappable MP David Lightbown felt that he had to do something to assuage his constituents. He therefore promised his Staffordshire electors that he would use his considerable influence as a government whip to get a health minister to address a local public meeting. David Mellor was approached and agreed to Lightbown's request. Mellor had an excellent grasp of his brief and Lightbown was confident that the Socialists, who were bound to attend the meeting, would all be sent packing.

The event was held in, of all places, a local cattle auction room and was chaired by the local bishop with a leading Labour councillor in attendance. Mellor arrived with a confident Lightbown to a packed and (mostly) hostile audience.

The bishop opened the meeting with some less than impartial remarks and Mellor's blood was up. The bishop then called on Mellor to address the crowd and invited him to mount the auctioneer's rostrum. Still fuming over the politically partial opening. Mellor started confidently. 'Now ladies and gentlemen,' he began '. . . it appears that I am tonight's auctioneer. Well, what am I offered for one second-hand bishop and one second-rate councillor?' The usually robust Lightbown, who had wanted to calm the situation, nearly fainted at Mellor's aggressive opening salvo.

Commenting on the abilities of a Tory Foreign Office Minister he served with, he was dismissive: 'She has a long reach but a short grasp.'

Although Mellor nearly always got the best of any slanging match, there was one memorable occasion when he was bettered. During the passage of the Sexual Offences Bill, Mellor turned on a backbench MP who was filibustering. He accused fellow Tory Matthew Parris (who is now the parliamentary sketchwriter for *The Times*) of 'conducting a debate with himself'. Parris shot back: 'Maybe I am. But one has to have some kind of an intellectual challenge in this place.'

Kenneth Clarke is a political bruiser who could easily have become the leader of the Conservative Party if he had been prepared to modify his views on Europe. But he was not willing to trim his sails and the parliamentary party voted instead for William Hague. Characteristically, he has said to those who have questioned his action: 'What is the point of being in politics at all if you cannot pursue your own beliefs?' Still showing no signs of modifying his views, he has recently described his own leader's policy on Europe as: 'Way out.'

And Clarke on fellow Tory Norman (now Lord) Lamont: 'On the subject of Europe, he talks paranoid nonsense.'

Attacking his successor as Chancellor of the Exchequer, Gordon Brown, for relaxing spending controls, he said in 1998: 'He has transformed from the Iron Chancellor to the Big-handed Chancellor, with uncontrolled spending in just about every department in Whitehall. He will end this Parliament short of taxation and short of economic growth. His cheering supporters may ring the bells today but they will wring their hands shortly hereafter.'

Again on Gordon Brown: 'He has based his politics on the "Dolly Parton School of Economics" – an unbelievable figure, blown out of all proportion, with no visible means of support.'

On New Labour: 'The idea of Labour backing business, keeping taxes low and reducing the deficit is completely absurd. It isn't just a matter of pigs flying, it's a whole farm-yard on a mission to deep space.'

On government generally: 'If I had to say which was telling the truth about society, a speech by a Minister of Housing, or the actual buildings put up in his time, I should believe the buildings.'

Commenting again on his successor: 'Gordon Brown, unlike previous Chancellors, cannot control interest rates. He is just a one-club golfer – but he has given the club away to the Governor of the Bank of England.'

And Clarke's view on Tony Blair's style: 'It's presidential. Blair enjoys the glittering style of the job. He enjoys the world stage. And he leaves hard-working chaps like Gordon Brown to go out and deliver the detail.'

John Redwood has a sharp intellect. He also had the courage to resign from the Conservative government and fight a leadership contest against John Major. This has led many Conservatives to resent him, if not for the former for the latter.

Accused of being an inflexible right-winger by some Conservatives, he retorted: 'I think in politics it is better to make up your mind and stick with it.'

On Peter Mandelson: 'There is only one project which preoccupies him. The Millennium dome. For Peter, Dome is where the heart it.'

Of Tony Blair, he said dismissively: 'He is a man who has no single political principle within him, who will change his views as often as opinion polls and spin doctors tell him to.'

Labour minister Ian McCartney has an ebullient and abrasive style in the Commons, although when he gets excited his Scottish brogue does tend to intensify to such an extent that one sometimes needs an interpreter. When pressed by Conservatives in the Commons, he usually launches into a tirade against the last government, frequently referring to the Tories as 'that lot'. When criticized himself he retorted: 'That Conservative rabble left us an appalling legacy. The best weapon against low pay is to see that that lot doesn't get elected again.'

Former Tory MP and junior Treasury Minister Phillip Oppenheim was an effective Commons performer and a clear asset to John Major's government during debate. However, when he started to miss a number of parliamentary votes at a time when Major's majority was down to almost zero, he became unpopular with the government Whips' office. Once, when a Tory MP asked Whip David Lightbown how he could contact Oppenheim, not having found him in the Commons chamber, he was bluntly told: 'You must realize Phillip Oppenheim is not just an MP but a minister in a government with a very very small Commons majority, where every vote counts. He can only be contacted either through his latest girlfriend, or down on his farm, or at Stringfellows or perhaps somewhere else in the country. If you find him, tell him we'd like him to vote once in a while. Now fuck off!'

Oppenheim's most effective barbs have actually been delivered outside the Commons chamber, where he has been more than lucky not to have been clobbered. After the *Sun* revealed that John Major's junior Transport Minister Steve Norris had been having affairs with no fewer than FIVE mistresses, Oppenheim took to calling him 'Knobber', and he has recently described Norris's post-election job, as head of the Road Haulage Federation, as a position which requires 'eating rubber chicken and Hirondelle with the truckies.'

On Labour's Gordon Brown MP: 'He does not deliver a speech, he delivers bile. However, we are entitled to ask, where is the beef?'

Oppenheim's view on Neil Kinnock: 'He is an obscure Welsh politician, best known for losing his rag with Zimbabwean soldiers and for nutting people in public lavatories.'

On former colleague David Evans, the straight-talking former

MP for Welwyn Harfield: 'He has a happy-clappy New Age attitude to life.'

He also refers to fellow Tory Edwina Currie as 'Gobby Eddie' adding: 'The one thing that unites the Conservative Party is hatred of Edwina.'

Just after Edwina had been forced to resign over the salmonella in eggs affair, I was dining with Phillip and fellow Tory Eric Forth. Forth ordered Eggs Benedict and when the dish arrived Oppenheim ordered Forth to wait and told him not to touch the food until he returned. He then walked the length of the Members' Dining Room and brought back Edwina on the pretext that Forth had wanted to see her. In front of the assembled table of guests Oppenheim inquired: "Right, Edwina, can Eric eat this?"' If looks could kill . . .

On fellow-conservative Ann Widdecombe MP, he is vicious: 'A thing from Planet Gross.'

On former Home Secretary Michael Howard: 'He looks like an Italian full-back about to cut your legs away.'

On former fellow MP Andrew Mitchell: 'Mr Slimeball.'

On leader of the Opposition William Hague: 'He promised to rebrand the Tories, a fresh start and an end of arrogance – then he appointed Brian Mawhinney to the front bench. Call me difficult but being prepared to die in the trenches in support of a hereditary second chamber and backing the recidivistic so-called Countryside Lobby may not be the best start for a party that needs to present itself as forward looking.'

On Lady Elspeth Howe of the Broadcasting Standards Commission, who is the wife of Tory peer Lord (Geoffrey) Howe: 'I am not sure why being out to pasture with a "dead sheep" for 45 years qualifies her to tell us what we can and cannot watch (on TV). But she says the public has a "right to redress". Damn right it does. It can switch the television off without her advice at £46,000 a year.'

Upsetting his own party, he has commented: 'General Hague and the Lightweight Brigade have got to start looking cuddly. Under Thatcher, the Conservatives were heartless but effective, while Labour was useless but nice. After Major, the Tories look both heartless and useless.'

On New Labour: 'It wants to be loved. So it has a focus group on almost everything. And where there is no focus group there are endless polls to fall back on. It tracks the daily ebb and flow of opinion and when it has locked on, it elbows its way to the head of the mob. It is easy to do when you have not got many convictions yourself.'

Of David Mellor he says: 'The media and sporting contacts he made as Heritage Secretary - some outside the boudoir - have stood him in good stead.'

But Labour's Scottish Secretary Donald Dewar has commented of Mr O: 'He is the kind of person who gives a public school education a bad name.'

Labour's Tony Banks is probably the most colourful character in the Labour Party. Before the election he gleefully described the former Tory Chancellor of the Exchequer, Ken Clarke, as someone who: 'In his usual arrogant and high-handed fashion, dons his Thatcherite jackboots and stamps all over local opinion. He is like Hitler with a beer belly.'

He is an avid fan of the theatre, unlike former Conservative backbencher Terry Dicks, who was opposed to public subsidy of the arts. Referring to Mr Dicks, Banks said: 'He is an unreconstructed Member of Parliament. When he leaves the chamber, he probably goes to vandalize a few paintings somewhere. He is to the arts what Vlad the Impaler was to origami. He gives us a laugh.'

And warming to his criticism of Mr Dicks, his favourite *bête noire* in the last Parliament: 'In arts debates, he plays the court jester. He has a muscular approach. He claims that the ballet is something for poofters in leotards. That is the level of his contribution. He is to the arts what the *Sun* is to English literature, or what the *A Team* is to embroidery.'

And bemoaning the fact that some Labour MPs also have little enthusiasm for the arts, he added: 'The Terry Dicks tendency is behind me as well as in front of me.'

During a debate on the advent of further television channels he winced: 'The thought of Edwina Currie coming at the public on ten different TV channels makes the strongest man balk.'

On former US President George Bush: 'He would not know a principle if it were stuck to the end of an Exocet and smashed straight through his head.'

On Margaret (now Lady) Thatcher: 'She is a half-mad old bag lady. The Finchley whinger. She said the poll tax was the government's flagship. Like a captain she went down with her flagship. Unfortunately for the Conservative Party, she keeps bobbing up again - her head keeps appearing above the waves.'

And expanding his views on Lady T: 'She is about as environmentally friendly as the bubonic plague. I would be happy to see Lady Thatcher stuffed, mounted, put in a glass case and left in a museum. She believes that anybody who opposed her - whether the Opposition or one of her friends - must by definition be wrong. She is a natural autocrat surrounded by a bunch of sycophants, many of whom have betrayed everything in which they once claimed to believe. She is far more influenced by the example of Attila the Hun than St Francis of Assisi. She is a petty-minded xenophobe who struts around the world interfering and lecturing in an arrogant and high-handed manner.'

On former Tory Environment Secretary the late Nicholas Ridley: 'Brutal, graceless and almost a complete waste of space.'

Former Labour MP Doug Hoyle was one day bemoaning the closure of British shipyards, arguing it would have been better if we had put them in mothballs. He then corrected himself and said that he would have preferred to have kept the shipyards open and instead put the then Trade of Industry Secretary Peter Lilley in mothballs. This led Tony Banks to gibe: 'They are the only balls he has.' Mr Hoyle agreed to bow to what he described as Mr Banks's superior knowledge of the minister's anatomy.

On another occasion, during a debate on conservation in the Antarctic, fellow Labour MP Peter Hardy pointed out that modern-day prospectors could do an enormous amount of damage in a small amount of time due to new technology. He illustrated his point by telling the House: 'Some people may imagine that a prospector is a hoary old man riding on a mule with a backpack of beans and dried bacon, hoping to extract a few bits of rocks with a hammer and a shovel and so discover gold.' At which Tony Banks interrupted: 'This sounds like Nicholas Ridley.'

Banks added later: 'Britain still has the reputation of being the dirtiest nation in Europe. That must have something to do with the raw sewage contained in Nicholas Ridley's speeches.

Commenting on John Major's performance on *Desert Island Discs* while Prime Minister: 'He should have chosen something from *The Beggar's Opera* because there is a whole chorus on the London streets which could join in.'

Again, on former PM John Major: 'He revealed himself as a

Thatcherite with a grin. He deserved to be called Tinkerbell as all he did was tinker with the problems of the British economy.'

On former Welsh Minister Nicholas Bennett: 'He has not actually practised sycophancy, because he is a natural sycophant.'

On former Chairman of the Tories 1922 Committee, Cranley Onlsow MP: 'A fine example of a political thug.'

On Michael Heseltine: 'His contributions to debates are as if the House was not made up of Members of Parliament, but of delegates, all with their blue rinses and red necks applauding to the rafters, rather similar to when he makes one of his speeches to the Conservative Party Conference.'

On former Food Minister Nicholas Soames: 'The amiable Crawley food mountain clearly likes his grub. At the Dispatch Box he could probably persuade MPs that arsenic is quite palatable if suitably chilled.'

On the last Conservative government: 'There is very little which is decent in this government of second-hand car salesmen, Arthur Daleys and low life generally – on second thoughts, I have probably been unfair to second-hand car salesmen.'

On the now defunct poll tax: 'It was a tax which was dreamt up by some halfwit in the Department of the Environment. A tax which was unfair, unloved and unclear – a good description of Margaret Thatcher's government.'

During a defence debate he snapped: 'when Conservatives describe weapons of death and destruction they become positively orgasmic. Looking at them, those are probably the only organisms that they are ever likely to have. Margaret Thatcher used to tremble with excitement at the thought of being able to press the nuclear button.'

On his own attitude to politics: 'I have always found it a great advantage to loathe my political opponents. It is not usually difficult, but John Major is not one of those that I loathe. How could I? We both grew up in Brixton. We both served as Lambeth councillors. We both like beans on toast. Where on this conjoined road of shared experiences did Major go so badly wrong and become a Tory? I think that it was when he got turned down for the job of bus conductor. He had his heart set on punching tickets and helping little old ladies on and off the bus, but he was spurned. At that point he vowed hideous revenge on us all, but to be able to get it he first had to push a little old lady from Finchley off the bus. Having achieved that, he has now turned his attention to the rest of us. Our fate is to be even more horrible than to be frog-marched out of Downing Street. We are to be buried alive under charters. I thought that the Citizen's Charter was just one document, but there are more and more charters in store.'

When interrupted by Conservative gibes he airily brushed them aside with: 'It appears that we are in the midst of a convention of small order waiters.'

On the Young Conservatives: 'It is the Tory Party equivalent of the Hitler Youth.'

On the state of Britain after eighteen years of Conservative government: 'Britain is heading pell-mell towards the status of a banana monarchy but without the benefits of bananas. The Tories have deliberately created mass unemployment as a policy. It is their way of trying to break the powers of the trade union movement and of forcing wages down. What Victorian values mean to Conservatives is that many of them would be quite happy to see little boys once again earning pennies by going up chimneys.'

And his conclusion: 'There are times when I find it difficult to work out whether the Conservative government is vicious or ignorant. I have come to the conclusion that it is both.'

On the House of Commons: 'Words are cheap in the House. In some cases, they are almost useless.'

Sometimes Banks's language is too rich. When former Foreign Office Minister Tim Sainsbury was answering questions, Tony Banks bawled at him: 'Yankee lickspittle.' One MP who was hard of hearing thought Banks was ordering a type of cream cake sold in one of Mr Sainsbury's stores. However, the barb was unparliamentary and was heard by the Speaker who promptly ordered Mr Banks to withdraw.

Comparing the difference in speeches between Labour's Tony Benn and former Tory MP Neil Hamilton, Banks commented: 'Comparing the two speeches is like comparing Demosthenes with Alf Garnett.' This led a Tory Whip to shout: 'Which is which?'

His view of the gentlemen of the press: 'The average journalist was not at the front of the queue when brains were being handed out.'

However, not all of his colleagues are fans of Mr Banks. Former fellow Labour MP Andrew Faulds described some of his contributions as 'puerile comments from an inevitably loquacious colleague.' Mr Faulds is not the only Socialist who has mixed feelings. During a lengthy speech Mr Banks expressed his disagreement with Tony Benn, who at the time was not in the chamber. Saying that he regarded Mr Benn's arguments as 'somewhat bankrupt', Mr Banks informed the House that he would ensure that his remarks were pointed out to Mr Benn 'as he probably does not spend a great deal of time reading my speeches – but then who does?' which led Labour-front-bencher Peter Snape to snipe: 'You do.' Displaying his knack of dispelling criticism from whatever quarter it emanates, Tony Banks responded: 'I most certainly do not bother to read my speeches because I know what a load of rubbish they are before anybody hears them.' No one in the House felt that they could argue with that!

However, it was not long after Labour's 1997 election victory that he went too far and got himself into trouble again during that year's Labour Party Conference, putting, for a short time at least, his own future in doubt.

On the same day that Tony Blair made his main address to the nation, Labour's *other* Tony caused a sensation when he lambasted Tories William Hague and Michael Portillo as well as his Labour colleague Peter Mandelson in a diatribe in highly dubious taste.

On 30 September, Mr Banks was one of half a dozen Labour ministers to address the left-wing Tribune Rally at the Corn Exchange in Brighton. Referring to the Conservative leadership election, Mr Banks said: 'And now to make matters worse, they have elected a foetus as party leader. I bet there's a lot of Tory MPs who wish they hadn't voted against abortion now.'

This attack was widely held to be unacceptable (not least because Banks had plagiarized an earlier, identical attack on Hague by actress Joan Collins!).

However, this was just for starters. Banks went on to claim that former Defence Minister Michael Portillo's plan for 'world domination' had come to grief on election night and he then likened him to Pol Pot, the former Khmer Rouge dictator, who has been blamed for the deaths of more than a million people.

Banks continued: 'At one moment Portillo was polishing his jackboots and planning the advance. And the next thing he shows up as a TV presenter. It is rather like Pol Pot joining the Teletubbies.'

He then turned on his colleague Peter Mandelson, comparing him to a figure out of *Dracula*. Mandelson had just failed to secure a seat on Labour's ruling National Executive Committee, having lost out to veteran left-wing MP Ken

Livingstone. He said those Labour Party members who had voted for Mr Livingstone should either 'not go out on their own at night – or take some garlic with them'. He seemed to be thoroughly enjoying himself as he then went on to suggest that Labour's Millbank headquarters – where the general election campaign was controlled – was 'making Mandelsons and storing them in the Millennium Dome at Greenwich' – the project then being overseen by Mandelson. He went on: 'And when the clock strikes midnight on December 31 1999, millions of Mandelsons will march from the Dome and civilization as we know it will be at an end.' These insults backfired badly and Banks was forced by party bosses to issue an immediate apology.

One Labour colleague has said that Banks 'has not yet made the transition from Labour Party court jester to Minister of the Crown'.

Although Banks was forced by Tony Blair to apologize for his attack on William Hague, he appears to have shown little remorse. Only a month later he told the *New Statesman* that he thought his own party's spin doctors had drawn attention to his remarks to deflect press criticism of comments made about the minimum wage at the same time by Peter Mandelson.

Despite his vitriolic tongue, Tony Banks is an articulate, intelligent, likeable and colourful character. Long may he remain active in British politics.

Former National Heritage Secretary Virginia Bottomley generally has a mild-mannered and emollient style, even when dealing with a troublesome opponent. However, on one memorable occasion she broke off from her speech to sing an insulting ditty to the Prime Minister. Announcing she had discovered a little-known Gilbert and Sullivan work called 'The Politicians' Song' from the operetta *Tony Blair*, to the tune of 'Ruler of the Queen's Navy' from *HMS Pinafore*, she sang:

'As a boy I went to public school
and learnt one very important rule,
If you say what people want to hear
your advancement soon will be very, very clear,
He used that rule so ruthlessly
that now he is the ruler of the Labour Party.

'In Islington some time he passed
and adopted all the manners of chattering class,
He drank white wine and he acted cool
and he sent his son to an opt-out school,
He went in style to Tuscany
and now he is the ruler of the Labour Party.

'Spin doctors rule, he dropped all thought,
he gagged John Prescott and he banned Clare Short,
Now he only says what people think is nice
and he offers you this piece of very wise advice:
"Just smile through your teeth and avoid policy
and you all could be rulers of the Labour Party".'

Fiery Old Labour MP Dennis Skinner, widely known as the 'Beast of Bolsover', is a formidable opponent. He attends debates regularly and has one of the best voting records in the House. He is also adept at the art of throwing speakers off their stride by a well-placed interruption or comment. On one occasion, when Margaret Thatcher rose for Prime Minister's Questions, he interjected: 'Here's the Westminster Ripper.'

Before the 1997 election, when former Heritage Secretary David Mellor rose to speak, Dennis Skinner caused much laughter by shouting: 'Here come swank.'

In July 1992 he was rather basic in his abuse when he insulted the Agricultural Minister John Gummer, calling him 'this little squirt of a minister'. This criticism upset the Speaker, Betty Boothroyd, who ordered Mr Skinner to withdraw his remarks. He refused and was ordered to leave the chamber for the rest of that day's sitting.

Commenting on John Gummer later, he showed no repentance, saying: 'He used to be the wart on Thatcher's nose.'

Towards the end of the John Major's time as Prime Minister, he started calling him a 'Ken Barlow replica', adding (and mixing his soaps): 'We ought to get John Major a walk-on part in a re-run of *Crossroads*.'

Commenting on Tory MP Phillip Oppenheim: 'A millionaire mammy's boy.'

On the Conservative leadership election, he opined: 'They turned out Margaret Thatcher like a dog in the night.' Earlier however, before the result of the challenge to Margaret Thatcher was known, a journalist eager to obtain a quote from an MP bumped into Skinner in the Commons corridor: 'What difference will it make if Michael Heseltine wins the Tory leadership race?' he inquired. 'None at all,' replied Skinner. Rather puzzled by this response, the journalist asked why. Dennis replied: 'Because they are both millionaires and both peroxide blondes.'

On the Major government: 'Tawdry and rotten.'

On why Parliament keeps such odd hours: 'The biggest obstacle to changing hours - perhaps to nine to five - is the fact that more than 200 MPs - mainly Tory Members - have moonlighting jobs, making money in the boardrooms and the law courts. They want to come to the House when it suits them.' This led to the response from Conservative David Harris: 'Dennis Skinner constantly talks rubbish. Most Conservative MPs work harder because we are members of committees. Dennis refused to serve on them.' And Tory Patrick Nicholls added: 'It is unusual to see Dennis Skinner in the chamber out of prime television time.'

On the Liberal Democrats: 'All they are interested in is getting round Paddy Backdown – otherwise known as Captain Mainwaring – so that this little Dad's Army can have a caucus meeting to discuss what their politics are at the General Election.'

During the 1992 General Election, when it was revealed that Mr Ashdown had had an affair, Mr Skinner started referring to the leader of the Liberal Democrats as 'Paddy Pantsdown'.

His name for David (now Lord) Owen: 'Dr Death'.

On business tycoon Richard Branson: 'He is Mr Goody Two-shoes.'

On the press: 'In Britain, there is no such thing as a free press, as most of it is owned by a clique of millionaires.'

Tory MP Sir Teddy Taylor received a colourful postbag when he announced that he had decided to support the Wild Animals (Protection) Bill, which would have outlawed foxhunting. He received one letter from a constituent saying he was 'consorting with Communists', and another saying he was 'supporting Socialist crackpots'. A further missive described him as a 'repulsive creep' – but he says: 'I didn't mind because I do not know what that is, but the most serious charge of all was the letter I had saying I was a "disgrace to the Monday Club".'

Former Labour front-bencher and now Select Committee Chairman, Gerald Kaufman, has an acid tongue and is generally extremely effective in debate. Once, after a speech by former MP Tim Smith, in which he loyally praised his own party's policies, Mr Kaufman snapped: 'I knew he had learnt to speak but I did not know he had learnt to crawl.'

Commenting on his former boss Harold Wilson: 'He is the only man I know who deliberately acquired a sense of humour.'

On the Conservative Party: 'When the Tories think they are facing electoral defeat they dive head-first into the political sewer. The 1945 Gestapo scare has its equivalent in the 1992 scare that Saddam Hussein might take a risk or two. The Tory bogeymen may change, but the Tory's lack of principle remains the same.'

On Nigel Lawson: 'His style is a mixture of bluster, smugness and arrogance.'

On former Tory Cabinet minister John Selwyn Gummer: 'A political pipsqueak.'

On John Major's government: 'They are particularly puny and petty. They brandish their nuclear weapons like some macho symbol.'

And on John Major and his predecessor: 'The thing about Mrs Thatcher was there was a character to assassinate. The problem with Mr Major is that you look and look – and where is it?'

Recently Mr Kaufman has found himself, somewhat unusually, to be on the receiving end. Tory backbenchers have unkindly taken to calling him 'Kermit'.

Former Tory Education Secretary John Patten on Labour MPs Barry Sheerman and Stuart Randall: 'We have here a couple of shellbacks – they are like two middle-aged mutant turtles.'

Junior Labour minister Peter Kilfoyle on Conservative front-bench spokesman Sir Patrick Cormack: 'By his own admission he is the patron saint of lost causes.'

And Kilfoyle on the Liberal Democrats: 'They have changed their name from the Liberals but I could suggest an even better name: the Party of Janus, because Liberal Democrats have the unique ability to face both ways at once.'

Labour's Barry Sheerman commenting on himself: 'I may or may not be a parliamentary poodle – but I am an unreconstructed Keynesian.'

Welsh back-bench Labour MP Paul Flynn, taking a rather basic swipe at former National Heritage Secretary David Mellor before the 1997 election, said: 'When he loses his seat, he can get an alternative job delivering gorillagrams without the aid of a monkey suit.'

Mr Flynn seems to have something of a penchant for primate-related belligerence. Of John Major's Welsh ministerial team he said: 'The three Tory Welsh Office ministers have become the three unwise monkeys of Wales who neither see, hear, nor talk of unemployment, but hide from it. Are they three monkeys or three cheetahs?'

Back-bench Tory MP Sir Peter Lloyd on Labour's former Deputy Leader Roy (now Lord) Hattersley: 'He has an imperfect grasp of what he is talking about, but he always has to fill his speeches with reports of famous victories. He likes to puff himself up like a bullfrog. He may impress some of his friends, but he looks risible to us.'

Labour Defence Secretary George Robertson on John Major's government: 'Most of their members have been forgotten, although their legacy lingers on.'

Just after he was elected to the House, former Tory Minister Sir Jeremy Hanley was surprised to find himself sitting next to the Reverend Ian Paisley MP. Hanley remarked: 'I didn't know you were on our side,' to which he received the retort from Paisley: 'Never confuse sitting on your side with *being* on your side.'

Health Secretary Frank Dobson has a down-to-earth approach. His view of the last Conservative government: 'They were so useless that they lost the last election by the biggest landslide in the twentieth century.'

His view of his opponents: 'I would not take the word of the Conservatives if they were the last people on earth.'

Dobson's opinion of leading Tory MP Ann Widdecombe is succinct: 'she's a cheapskate,"

Meanwhile Miss Widdecombe, disputing Dobson's claims about the health service, has taken to referring to him as 'Fiddling Frank'.

And, on the record of the New Labour government: 'The first Labour promise was, "We will stick to the previous government's spending plans." Their second promise was, "We will reduce hospital waiting lists." The Labour Party made twin promises at the same time and yet they now have the nerve to blame keeping one promise for breaking the other.'

Before he was defeated at the 1992 General Election, Nicholas Bennett, the Tory MP for Pembroke, was involved in an accident on a motorway when his car overturned. Miraculously he was not injured. Although there was no suggestion that the accident was his fault, one colleague quipped: 'Nick Bennett drives so fast that if a vehicle is not travelling at over 60 miles per hour, he thinks it's a house.'

When Bennett was serving on the Standing Committee considering the NHS and Community Care Bill, Labour spokesman, now minister, Alun Michael started to speak to an amendment on the availability of drugs. Although the issue could have been disposed of quickly, Michael spoke slowly and at length. To much Labour annoyance, Bennett interjected saying that he 'hoped there would soon be plenty of drugs available to cure verbal diarrhoea.'

Bennett on Labour MP Alice Mahon: 'The Madam Defarge of the Labour Party.'

Commenting on the amount of public backing enjoyed by the Liberal Democrats: 'The current level of electoral support for the Liberal Democrats would be impressive only if it was measured on the Richter scale.'

Promoted to Junior minister at the Welsh Office in 1991, Bennett usually packed a punch at Welsh questions and he became known for his combative style. On one occasion I met him just before his question time and he asked me if I knew of any good insults which he might be able to use as he was expecting to be attacked by a vociferous group of Welsh Labour MPs. Flippantly I replied: 'You could say that the trouble with the Welsh is that they ought to stop singing and get some coal up.'

During questions Bennett was not quite his usual self and turned in a fair but somewhat subdued performance. We met afterwards and he exploded. 'You bastard!' he said. 'That gibe of yours stuck in my mind and I was so worried that I might blurt it out, I could not concentrate on anything else.'

When it was announced during the summer of 1990 that Tory back-bencher Michael Latham, who held the safe seat of Melton, had decided to retire early and give up politics for the Church, Bennett quipped: 'If you become a grocer, you get groceries for nothing; if you become a newsagent you read the papers for nothing; if you become a politician, you speak for nothing; but if you become a preacher, you get good for nothing.'

Shortly after he lost his Welsh seat at the 1992 election, Mr Bennett returned to the Commons to clear his desk. As he was leaving he was approached by a tourist who appeared to be lost and rather confused. 'Excuse me sir, can you tell me the quickest way out of this place?' she inquired. His reply was terse: 'Certainly, madam. Stand as a Conservative candidate in Pembroke.'

Scottish Labour back-bencher Maria Fyfe commenting on Tory MP and front-bencher spokesman Michael Howard: 'He oozes insincerity from every pore. He strikes me as a man for whom the word "synthetic" would be a compliment because at least some synthetic things can be capable of useful service.'

Former deputy leader of the Conservative Party Peter Lilley recently explained the difference between a New Labour back-bench MP and a supermarket trolley: 'A supermarket trolley has a mind of its own,' he said derisively.

And on New Labour's tax policies: 'An interesting illusion. They have raised taxes massively with their left hand and given back a small amount with their right hand.'

Commenting on Labour's former Paymaster General Geoffrey Robinson: 'He is well-known for dodging answering questions about either his own taxes or the taxes that he is imposing on others.

On the Prime Minister: 'Tony Blair recently visited China. It's a place where he feels at home. It's the only place where they are as tough on dissent as they are in the Labour Party.'

In 1998, Mr Lilley claimed to have found the sheet music to a New Labour Version of *Land of Hope and Glory*, which he claimed had been renamed '*Land of Pseudo Tories*.' The lyrics, to the original tune, he claims are as follows:

> *Land of chattering classes*
> *No more pageantry*
> *Darlings, raise your glasses*
> *To brave modernity.*
> *Who needs Nelson or Churchill?*
> *The past is so passé*
> *Britain's now about Britpop and the River café*
> *God, this place is so frumpy*
> *Let's be more like LA.*

Following the shock resignation of Peter Mandelson MP as Secretary of State for Trade and Industry early in 1998, when news of his massive home loan from Geoffrey Robinson MP became public knowledge, Lilley quipped: 'We now discover that the man who threw the most stones was living in the most expensive glasshouse in London.'

Only two months after Labour's 1997 election victory, Labour MP Ken Livingstone fired a warning shot at Blair's style of government, saying: 'The discipline of Labour's left in the election was absolute, but we cannot be expected to remain silent as we watch the government sow the seeds of a future Labour General Election defeat.'

Former Home Office Minister and Euro-politician Tim Kirkhope is a classic car fan. He owns a Porsche 911 and, like most car enthusiasts, he enjoys driving rather than bragging about his car ownership. Once he was confronted with a particularly pompous businessman who was boasting about his own cars and who managed to bring each vehicle he owned into every aspect of the conversation. Eventually the bore started to talk about his own Porsche and pointed out that the following week he intended to 'travel to London with the 911'. Kirkhope silenced him with the barb: 'Yes, I often catch it myself from Newcastle Central.'

Commenting on Ann Widdecombe MP; 'She has such a sharp tongue, that she often risks cutting her own throat.'

Home Secretary Jack Straw on his former Conservative

shadow, Norman Fowler: 'He speaks in tongues of double-talk, saying one thing one day and another the next.'

Tim Wood, the usually placid former MP for Stevenage, commenting on his successor, the four times married Mrs Barbara Follett MP: 'She has been more successful in politics than in love. It has only taken her three attempts to reach the House of Commons.'

Welsh Minister Alun Michael, after being attacked in debate by Tory MP John Bercow: 'He is a case of a backbench Member being tough on the English language and soft on his thinking.'

Veteran Labour MP Brian Sedgemore showed that he has little time for the 1997 intake of New Labour women MPs, whom he appears to regard as mere lobby fodder. Early in 1998 he surprised those attending a meeting at the Tate Gallery with the gibe: 'These New Labour women MPs are like the *Stepford Wives* with a chip inserted into their brain to keep them on-message.'

However, at least one of Labour's women MPs has proved herself a good match for Mr Sedgemore. Labour Whip Bridget Prentice approached him when he indicated he was going to vote against his own party on single-parent benefits and cooed: 'If I though you had goolies, I'd crush them.'

Tory Simon Burns MP on former Labour back-bencher Martin Flannery: 'He's the unthinking man's Alf Garnett.'

New Labour MP Jim Murphy on the House of Lords: 'It is the single largest regular gathering of pensioners in Britain.'

Tory Tim (now Lord) Renton was rather a good Arts Minister under John Major and he proved to be one of the few politicians to better Labour's Dennis Skinner. When, asking an arts question, the Bolsover MP inquired of him: 'How many civil servants are (a) men or (b) women?' Mr Renton tersely replied: 'All of them.'

Former Labour Deputy Leader Roy Hattersley on Tony Blair's style of government: 'The Cabinet meets now for thirty minutes on a Thursday morning. Tony is very near to giving Cabinet government a lethal injection.'

Tory Gary Streeter MP on Labour Minister Clare short MP: 'She has fully met her vitriol quota.'

Fiery Labour MP Diane Abbott says of Blair's New Labour government: 'It's a *Boy's Own* project – a highly centralized government – and it's all men.'

Tory back-bencher and diarist Alan Clark is always worth listening to, as an insult or put-down is never far below the surface. While a minister, he caused a furore by referring to one African state as 'Bongo Bongo land'.

On the media: 'The power of television has become fearsome and it is now being abused. TV is staffed by limousine liberals.'

When he was particularly rude towards Edwina Currie, Mrs C said: 'Oh Alan, don't be so nasty,' to which he retorted: 'Ask around my dear, I am nasty.'

Widely known as an historian, when he was asked: 'Where did you read history?', he snapped back: 'In an armchair.'

Commenting on English Heritage: 'English Heritage has got too big for its boots. Its director is a prominent figure in what is sometimes referred to as café society and he is seen enjoying hospitality in many locations.'

His ability to startle is undimmed. In 1998, when politicians from all parties and also the press were united in their condemnation of English soccer hooligans in Marseilles, Clark came to their defence, saying: 'English football fans have become the targets of everyone from ordinary police to known Mafia enforcers from Argentina,' adding: 'Football matches are now the substitute for medieval tournaments and it's perfectly natural that some of the fans should be obstreperous.' He didn't leave it there and went on to attack his own party's proposals to restrict the fans' freedom to travel, saying that Shadow Home Secretary Norman Fowler's plans were: 'Unconservative and completely illegal wartime restrictions on people's movements.'

Local Government Minister Hilary Armstrong is not normally offensive but during a recent lively debate on proposals to cap Derbyshire County Council, held during the football World Cup, she infuriated Conservative MPs by accusing them of having a 'similar mentality to soccer hooligans', adding that they had shown the 'sort of behaviour which brings this country into disrepute.'

Former Cabinet Minister Michael Portillo recently attacked the policies of New Labour and accused Tony Blair of adopting 'a karaoke Conservatism', adding: 'Unlike Tony Blair, William Hague doesn't over-promise. He favours sentences over soundbites and joined up thoughts over disjointed platitudes.'

Tory MP Nick St Aubyn got himself into hot water in 1999 when he took what was seen as a sexist swipe at Payment General Dawn Primarolo. The MP for Guildford quipped that she was just the kind of minister to: 'lie back and think of Europe.'

Veteran Labour MP Tony Benn on the House of Lords: 'A chamber elected by nobody and accountable to nobody.'

And on the New Labour government of Tony Blair: 'The government has no industrial policy and seems to have made protection of the rich one of its main objectives.'

Former Tory Chancellor Norman (now Lord) Lamont on PM Tony Blair: 'Blair is "presentation, presentation, presentation – and nothing but presentation".'

Back-bench Labour MP Derek Wyatt on his own party: 'I do not believe in the growing Napoleonic centralist control of the Parliamentary Labour Party. This smacks of 1984.'

Lord Coggan shocked quite a few when he criticized both the frenzy surrounding the death of Diana, Princess of Wales, and the Princess herself. He recently said: 'Britain has become godless. Man is made with a hollow which only God can fill. Then along came this false goddess and filled the gap for a time. But, like all false gods, she could not last.' He then added: 'The British people identified with someone who had pretty loose morals and certainly loose sexual morals. A period of disillusionment is bound to set in.'

Like any other employer, a Member of Parliament occasionally finds the need to dismiss staff. Some employees, who see it coming, leave of their own volition, just ahead of dismissal. One particular MP, who was delighted when an incompetent researcher finally moved on, provided the following reference: 'He has worked for me for over a year and when he left, I was completely satisfied.'

And, in a similar vein, another wrote: 'She has worked for me now for over six months, completely to her own satisfaction.'

Labour Minister Brian Wilson is generally hard-hitting in debate. The north-of-the-border MP usually packs quite a punch, although this is often diluted by his frequent use of what can only be described as the Scottish version of the 'um' and the 'er' – a sort of 'eeaaaarrrrgh'. When Wilson heard that SNP leader Alex Salmond had decided to promote his former chauffeur, Stewart Stevenson, to a list of candidates for the Scottish Parliament despite the fact that Stevenson had been previously rejected by the selection panel, his response was typical: 'Caligula appointed his horse as a consul of Rome and Salmond helps his driver. It confirms just how much of a one-man band the SNP is.'

The Leader of the SNP Alex Salmond frequently takes a swipe at the present Labour government. Commenting on New Labour's Economic Policy, he said recently: 'The only way to run a small business in Gordon Brown's economy is to start with a big business.'

Anonymous on Scotland's First Minister, Donald Dewar MSP: 'His nose is enormous. It stabs at the Conservatives as though they were whelks to be pickled.'

And again on Mr Dewar: 'He has an endearing attachment to rectitude.'

Former Conservative Minister Lord James Douglas-Hamilton has said of Mr Dewar 'He has the capability to exhaust time and encroach upon eternity.'

Former Liberal-Democrat Leader Paddy Ashdown was quite effective when commenting on the Conservatives during the 1999 Euro-elections: 'The only think you need to know about the modern Tory Party is that Dr Alan Sked* can vote for them, Ian Gilmour** won't vote for them and Jonathan Aitken*** cannot vote for them.'

Former Conservative Foreign Secretary Sir Malcolm Rifkind on what it's like to lose ministerial office: 'You suddenly realize that you are no longer in government when you get into the back of your car and it doesn't go anywhere.'

The only independent MP in the Commons is Martin Bell, who defeated Tory Neil Hamilton at the 1997 General Election. He recently said of his position: 'I am the eighth largest party in the House of Commons', later adding: 'Of course, mine is the first Party Conference of the season – it's all party and no conference.'

---

* Former Leader of UK Independence Party.
** Former Conservative Cabinet Minister, widely regarded as a 'wet'. Sacked by Mrs Thatcher, and now Lord Gilmour.
*** Former Conservative Cabinet Minister, sent to prison for perjury in June 1999.

INSULTS
FROM ACROSS
THE ATLANTIC

As the democratic political system of the United States of America is based on the British model, it is not surprising to find that its elected members spend a similar amount of time trading insults as their British counterparts.

Certainly the American public appear to hold their politicians in the same esteem. It was Mark Twain who wrote: 'Suppose you were an idiot and suppose you were a member of Congress – but I repeat myself.'

American humorist Will Rogers, a somewhat gentler observer, described politicians as 'a never-ending source of amusement, amazement and discouragement'. He went on to add: 'Congress has promised the country that it will adjourn next Tuesday. Let's hope we can depend on it. If they do, it will be the first promise they have kept.'

However, grumbles from the public, whinges from journalists and cracks from comedians, all pale into insignificance compared with the vitriol politicians use against each other.

President John Quincy Adams on George Washington: 'Not a scholar. That he is too illiterate, unlearned, unread for his station and reputation, is equally beyond dispute.'

Of one former South Carolina Congressman named Rivers an opponent quipped: 'I never knew that Mendel Rivers drank until I saw him sober.'

The first women to become members of Congress in the USA were regarded as something of a curiosity. In the 1920s Speaker Longworth called them 'gentlewomen'. They were, however, subject to much teasing. On one occasion when a female member of Congress tried to intervene in a debate, she was dismissed by the Congressman who held the floor with: 'Not now - it's not often that a man is in a position to make a woman sit down and keep quiet.'

No one could keep Alice Roosevelt Longworth quiet for long. Commenting on politician Thomas Dewey in 1948 she inquired: 'Does a soufflé rise twice?'

And on Warren Harding she observed: 'He was not a bad man - he was just a slob.'

Clare Booth Luce was vitriolic about former Governor George Wallace of whom she said: 'What he calls his global thinking is, no matter how you slice it, still "globaloney".'

During the 1950s Republican Senator Wayne Morse decided to leave the Republican Party and join the Democrats. Clare Booth Luce silenced him with the barb: 'Whenever a Republican joins the Democrats, it raises the intelligence quotient of both parties.'

It is not only bile and venom that over the years have

threatened the good order of debate. In the nineteenth century Massachusetts Senator Daniel Webster often imbibed too freely before making a speech. On one occasion he was in such a bad state as he was due to speak that a friend sitting behind him agreed to help him through the ordeal. As Webster stood wavering after his opening remarks, the Senator sitting behind him whispered 'tariff'. It seemed to do the trick and Webster gathered his thoughts and proceeded to speak for a couple of minutes on the subject. Then he began to sway and nod. 'National debt' prompted his friend again. Again, Webster was able to continue: 'Gentlemen, then there's the national debt – it should be paid.' At this point loud cheers broke out in the chamber which roused Webster. 'Yes, gentlemen,' he repeated himself. 'It should be paid.' This produced even louder cheers, at which point Webster seemed to have forgotten what he was talking about. 'And I'll be damned,' he said, taking out his cheque book, 'I'll pay it myself. How much is it?' At this, any bad temper that his drunken ramblings were arousing completely dissolved into loud laughter as Webster was always broke. He then collapsed into his chair and promptly fell asleep.

However, this amusing but rather disgraceful episode appears to have been the exception as far as Webster was concerned. Many contemporaries have commented that Webster was one of the few politicians who could speak effectively even when completely drunk. Indeed, many young politicians concluded that Webster did his best work 'while under the influence' and some of them drank to excess in the hope of becoming as fluent.

Webster was an extremely clever orator who frequently used invective for effect. When a colleague named John Trout made an assertion which Webster did not believe, he started to refer to Trout as an 'amphibious animal'. After a while Trout became inquisitive and asked Webster precisely what he meant by this remark. Webster turned to his one-time friend and said: 'It means, John, an animal that lies equally well on land and on water.'

A Virginia Senator called William Archer became the source of amusement to many of his colleagues for his preference for long-winded vocabulary. He was not a particularly good orator and for effect he used obscure, long words. The result of this was that his speeches were almost incomprehensible.

Daniel Webster's style was completely opposite, as he realized that a good orator had to be understood by even the slowest of audiences. A colleague from South Carolina one day asked Webster what he thought of Senator Archer. 'He's too fond of grandiloquence,' Webster said. 'What precisely do you mean?' the politician asked. 'Well I dined with Archer today and I think he is a preposterous aggregation of heterogenous paradoxes and perdurable peremptorences!'

Republican Senator Reed Smoot of Utah did not think much of British author D. H. Lawrence. Having read *Lady Chatterley's Lover*, he described Lawrence as 'a man with a soul so black that he would even obscure the darkness of hell'.

However, Smoot's aim to continue the ban on the book he regarded as obscene failed, causing a more liberal senator to remark: 'The United States has been officially lifted out of the infant class.'

Smoot used to tell of the incident when one of his pompous colleagues was in a Washington hotel being shaved by an old black barber who had seen many Senators come and go through the years. The pompous politician said to the barber: 'You must have had many of my distinguished predecessors in your chair.'

'Yes,' answered the barber. 'I've known most of them and you remind me of Daniel Webster.'

The politician beamed with pride. 'Is it my profile or my speeches that remind you of him?' he inquired.

'Neither,' said the barber. 'It's your bad breath.'

During a particularly amusing debate in Congress, members of the public in the gallery started laughing so loud that it disrupted the proceedings. The presiding officer threatened to clear the galleries if the noise didn't cease, when Senator Alben Barkley rose apparently to plead on behalf of the public, saying: 'I do not think that the Chair ought to be too hard on the galleries. When people go to a circus, they ought to be allowed to laugh at the monkey.'

This not only caused more laughter, but was quite a clever way of throwing an insult towards Senator Huey Long, who was speaking at the time.

Former Kentucky Senator Alben Barkley, who was Harry Truman's vice-president, had been happily married for many years when he was asked what his formula was for a successful marriage. He replied: 'My wife and I have an agreement that she makes all the small decisions and I make all the big ones.' 'And have you ever argued?' a journalist asked. 'Never,' he replied, later adding: 'But then, we have never had to make a big decision.'

The Chairman of the Aluminium Association of America was not a Barkley fan and he found an effective way of deflating the vice-president after Barkley had made a prepared speech to the Association. Barkley thought he had done quite well but the Chairman rose from his seat and told the audience:

'I have three criticisms. In the first place, you read your speech. In the second place, you read it poorly. And in the third place, it wasn't worth reading,' before disappearing out of the door.

During one particular debate, North Carolina's Senator Robert Reynolds, who was known for his long-windedness, was rambling on about the fascinating places he had visited around the world. The leader of the Senate, Mr Barkley, was anxious to conclude the business and sat there listening impatiently. Eventually Reynolds moved on to the beauties of the Far West and started describing the islands in the Pacific. At this point Barkley interrupted him and said: 'Senator, please, let us off when you get to Changhai.'

On another occasion Senator Barkley was asked what made a wise Senator. He replied: 'To have good judgement. Good judgement comes from experience,' whereupon a student in the audience asked him what experience came from. Barkley's response: 'Well, that comes from bad judgement.'

Over the decades a number of Congressmen have had a drinking problem. During one particularly boozy Congress where many of the elected representatives drank heavily, one politician posed a congressional riddle, namely: 'What is the difference between a discussion and a fight?' The answer: 'Six bourbons.'

Jenkin Lloyd Jones gave some advice which many politicians today would do well to heed. On a political oration he said: 'It is a solemn responsibility. The man who makes a bad thirty-minute speech to 200 people wastes only half an hour of his own time. But he wastes 100 hours of the audience's time – more than four days – which should be a hanging offence.'

In 1811 Kentucky representative Henry Clay silenced Virginia Congressman John Randolph who had said Clay wasn't paying any attention to his speeches. Clay shot back: 'You are mistaken. I will wager that I can repeat as many of your speeches as you can.' This silenced Randolph for the rest of the week.

Alexander Smyth was a long-winded bore. In the middle of one of his long speeches he noticed fellow Congressman Henry Clay getting restless and said: 'You may speak for the present generation, but I speak for posterity.' To which Clay replied: 'Yes, and you seem resolved to continue speaking until your audience arrives.'

Republican Senator Chauncey Depew, an extremely large man, was challenged as to why he did not do more exercise. He retorted: 'I get my exercise acting as a pall-bearer to my friends who exercise.'

One evening Depew found that he was due to speak at a dinner after the great wit Mark Twain. Twain spoke first and received a tremendous ovation when he sat down. Depew rose to his feet and said: 'Ladies and gentlemen, before this dinner Mark Twain and I made an agreement to trade speeches. He has just delivered my speech and I thank you for the pleasant manner in which you have received it. I regret to say that I have lost the notes of Mr Twain's speech and I cannot remember anything he had to say.' He then sat down.

In 1894 Congressman O'Neill from Missouri was interrupted during a speech and he was so furious he snapped back: 'If the gall which you have in your heart could be poured into your stomach, you'd die instantly of the black vomit.'

In the last century Virginia Senator John Randolph was one of the most striking figures to appear in Congress. He used to ride to Capitol Hill and enter the chamber with riding whip in hand and a small cap on his head. He was unpredictable – and usually very insulting.

On one occasion a man who had met him at dinner a couple of days earlier saw him walking to the Capitol, rushed over to him and said: 'Good morning, Mr Randolph – how do you do?' Good morning,' Randolph replied without stopping or looking up. The man continued: 'You walk very fast, Mr Randolph, and I have great difficulty in keeping up with you.' Randolph snapped back: 'In that case, I'll increase the difficulty,' and he hurried off.

He was an ardent supporter of President Jefferson for most of his career, but he thought President John Quincy Adams was useless. He once met an Adams supporter on a narrow pavement. The man stopped in front of Randolph, completely blocking his way and said to him belligerently: 'I never step out of my way for puppies!' 'Oh, I always do,' said Randolph as he stepped aside. 'Please pass.'

In 1824 Henry Clay threw his support behind John Quincy Adams in the election of that year. After Adams's victory, he was made Secretary of State. Incensed, Randolph spoke of a 'corrupt bargain' between the two and, addressing the House in 1826, talked about 'the alliance – offensive and defensive' between the two men, later referring to their friendship as a deal between 'a puritan and a blackleg'. Clay deeply resented being called a blackleg, which meant a crooked gambler, and actually challenged Randolph to a duel. This incident, however, ended happily as when they fired their shots in the duel, both missed, and then made up their quarrel.

Towards the end of life, he became somewhat senile, frequently tearing up his papers in sudden outbursts of anger. He directed that when he died he was to be buried facing west so that he could keep an eye on Henry Clay whose nationalist views he detested.

During one debate he called President John Quincy Adams 'a traitor', then he called Daniel Webster 'a vile slanderer', and referred to John Holmes as 'a dangerous fool'. He called another colleague 'the most contemptible and degraded of beings, who no man ought to touch, unless with a pair of tongs.'

However, Randolph did get his come-uppance. He had rather a high-pitched voice which caused Congressman Burges to snipe: 'He is impotent of everything but malevolence of purpose.'

Sometimes Randolph could be amusing. Of two congressional colleagues, Robert Wright and John Rae, he said: 'The House exhibits two anomalies – a Wright always wrong, and a Rae without light.'

He effectively insulted Congressman Samuel Dexter, a politician who had shifted his views on a number of issues: 'Mr Ambi-Dexter.'

On power he said: 'Power alone can limit power.'

On being in politics: 'It gives us that most delicious of all privileges – spending other people's money.'

He also said: 'Time is at once the most valuable and the most perishable of all our possessions.

Randolph coined a number of *bons mots* among which the following are the most memorable:

'Asking the United States to surrender part of her sovereignty is like asking a lady to surrender part of her chastity.'

'We all have two educations: one which we receive from others and another – and the most valuable – which we give ourselves.'

Ben Butler was a Republican candidate for Congress in the 1860s. During a political rally in New York he encountered much heckling which threatened to disrupt his speech. Suddenly an apple was thrown in his direction and hit him on the head. Butler at once pulled out a knife and some of the people in the front row were frightened that he was going to start slashing out at the demonstrators near the stage. Instead, he bent over, picked up the apple, peeled it and began eating it. The crowd became quiet and Butler commented: 'Mmm, not a bad apple that.' He was cheered and then continued his speech in perfect silence.

Butler was extremely long-winded and would usually fill his speeches with references to his military exploits during the American Civil War. This led to one of his colleagues saying: 'Every time Ben Butler opens his mouth, he puts his feats in it.'

Of course some insults can be unintentional. Benjamin Tillman used to represent South Carolina in the Senate. His most striking distinguishing feature was that he had a very bad cast in his left eye. One day he asked a new Senate page boy the name of a recently elected Senator sitting on the Republican side of the chamber. Unfortunately the page boy not only didn't know who the Republican Senator was, he did not know Tillman either. The page boy left Tillman and went over to the Senate clerk and asked: 'Who is the man with one eye?' Without looking up, the clerk replied: 'Cyclops'. The page boy rushed back to Tillman and said: 'Now, Senator Cyclops, I will go and find out the other Senator's name.' For once Tillman was speechless.

Democratic Senator Henry Ashurst of Arizona didn't think much of his electorate. His attitude was: 'When I have to choose between voting for the people or for special interest groups, I always help the special interest. They remember. The people forget.'

American political campaigner Edgar Watson Howe coined a number of *bons mots* and the following are among his best:

'Some people never have anything except ideals.'

'He belongs to so many benevolent societies that he is destitute.'

'If you think before you speak, the other fellow gets his joke in first.'

'No man's credit is as good as his money.'

'One of the difficult tasks in this world is to convince a woman that even a bargain costs money.'

'The most natural man in a play is the villain.'

'Financial sense is knowing that certain men will promise to do certain things, and fail.'

'Express a mean opinion of yourself occasionally; it will show your friends that you know how to tell the truth.'

'A modest man is usually admired - if people ever hear of him.'

'Many a man is saved from being a thief by finding everything locked up.'

'The way out of trouble is never as simple as the way in.'

Ohio Congressman Thomas Corwin was an effective speaker in the 1840s. He was once cornered by a pompous colleague who began bragging about how he was a better orator than Corwin, and then started reciting long passages from some of the speeches he had given. The bore went on to say: 'If I didn't have so many irons in the fire, I'd publish every one of my speeches for posterity.' He got the response he deserved from Corwin: 'Take my advice, Senator, and put your speeches where your irons are.'

American President Abraham Lincoln, who was assassinated in 1865, is well known as a civil rights campaigner. However, he also had a barbed tongue. Of a colleague he remarked: 'He can compress the most words into the smallest idea better than any man I ever met.'

His view on slavery: 'What kills a skunk is the publicity it gives itself.'

And, in replying to an admirer who sent him a copy of a first edition, he gave the delightfully equivocal reply: 'Be sure that

I shall lose no time in reading the book which you have sent me.'

In 1858 when Lincoln was standing for the Senate against Stephen Douglas, he said of his opponent: 'When I was a boy I spent considerable time sitting by the river. An old steamboat came by, the boiler of which was so small that when they blew the whistle, there wasn't enough steam to turn the paddle wheel. When the paddle wheel went around, they couldn't blow the whistle. My opponent, Mr Douglas, reminds me of that old steamboat, for it is evident that when he talks he can't think and when he thinks he can't talk.'

When he was asked to comment on the weight of his adversary Stephen Douglas' argument, he said: 'It is thin as the homeopathic soup that was made by boiling the shadow of a pigeon that had starved to death.'

On later being called a 'two-faced politician' by the said Mr Douglas, he replied: 'I leave the answer to my audience – if I had another face to wear, do you think I would wear this one?'

During the election Douglas and Lincoln held a number of debates in various parts of Illinois.

During one of them Douglas made continual references to Lincoln's lowly origins, and in one particular speech he said that the first time he'd met Lincoln was across the counter of a general store where Lincoln was selling whisky. Realizing that there were temperance people in the audience, Douglas added: 'and he was an excellent bartender too'. Thinking he'd got the better of his opponent, he sat down. Lincoln rose to his feet and capped Douglas's comments with this reply: 'What my opponent says is true. I did keep a general store and sometimes sold whisky. I particularly remember Mr Douglas as he was a very good customer. Many a time I have been on one side of the counter selling whisky to Mr Douglas who was on the other side. But now, here's the difference between us – I have left my side of the counter, but he sticks to his.'

Although he won the argument that night, Lincoln lost the election. When the result was declared, he said he felt 'like the boy who stubbed his toe', adding: 'I am too big to cry, and too badly hurt to laugh.'

At a function when his host mentioned a local historian and enthused: 'I doubt whether any of our generation has plunged more deeply into the sacred fount of learning,' Lincoln, who was not impressed, snapped: 'Yes, or come up drier.'

Asked by a journalist who his grandfather was, he snapped back: 'I don't know who my grandfather was. I am much more concerned to know what his grandson will be.'

On one occasion he ignored a snide remark by a colleague and actually went out of his way to be polite. Later a friend asked why he had not dispatched the political foe and Lincoln explained: 'Am I not destroying an enemy when I make a friend of him?'

He later developed this philosophy further, adding: 'A drop of honey catches more flies than a gallon of gall. So with men. If you would win a man to your cause, first convince him that you are his sincere friend. Therein is a drop of honey which catches his heart, which, say what he will, is the high road to his reason.'

He did not think much of the refreshment provided on Capitol Hill. To one of the waiters he barked: 'If this is coffee, please bring me some tea; but if this is tea, please bring me some coffee.'

Of his electorate: 'It has been my experience that people who have no vices have very few virtues.'

On being accused of breaking an election pledge: 'Bad promises are better broken than kept.'

On a political colleague: 'He reminds me of the man who murdered both his parents and then, when sentence was about to be pronounced, pleaded for mercy on the grounds that he was an orphan.'

On being asked how long he held a grudge, he said: 'I choose always to make my statute of limitations a short one.'

On women: 'A woman is the only thing I am afraid of that I know will not hurt me.'

Asked what political tact was, he replied: 'The ability to describe others as they see themselves.'

Among his other sayings, the following are the best:

'No man has a good enough memory to make a successful liar.'

'I don't think much of a man who is not wiser today than he was yesterday.'

'I can make brigadier-general in five minutes, but it is not easy to replace a hundred and ten horses.'

'The best thing about the future is that it comes only one day at a time.'

'Nearly all men can stand adversity, but if you want to test a man's character, give him power.'

His rebuttal of Socialism has stood the test of time, being frequently quoted to great effect by President Reagan in the 1980s: 'You cannot strengthen the weak by weakening the strong. You cannot help the wage-earner by pulling down the wage-payer. You cannot help the poor by destroying the rich. You cannot help men permanently by doing for them what they could and should do for themselves.'

When attacked for being a 'Conservative', he replied: 'Well, what is conservatism? Is it not adherence to the old and tried against the new and untried?'

During the Civil War Pennsylvania Congressman Thaddeus Stevens said that he thought that the War Minister Simon Cameron was a 'consummate scoundrel'. His friend queried what he meant, saying: 'Surely you don't think that Cameron would steal?' Stevens thought about the matter and replied: 'Well, I don't think he would steal a red-hot stove.' President Lincoln came to hear of the gibe, liked it, and repeated it himself on several occasions.

Sometimes an insult can be used by a politician to get himself out of a highly embarrassing situation. Once, when Washington Democrat Senator Henry Jackson was campaigning, he fell through a rotten stage floor and the audience started laughing at his predicament. He turned the situation to his advantage by quickly clambering back to the microphone and quipping: 'I was obviously standing on one of the planks from the Republican platform.'

Former President Thomas Jefferson was right on the button when commenting about his office: 'No man shall ever bring out of the Presidency the reputation which carries him into it.'

In December 1889 Maine's representative Thomas Reed became Speaker of the House and soon came to be respected for his forceful but fair rulings.

One day when his integrity was questioned by Richard Townsend, the Congressman from Illinois, Reed announced to the House: 'There are only two sets of people whose opinions I respect. My constituents, who know me, and the House, who knows Townsend. It is hardly necessary to say, therefore, that I stand vindicated before both.'

Reed also showed that he had a sense of humour. He once sent a telegram to members of the House demanding their presence for a sitting as he was concerned to see that a quorum was achieved. One Congressman who was held up by a flood which had washed away half of the railway line telegraphed back: 'Washout on the line. Can't come.' Reed immediately sent a telegram back: 'Buy a new shirt and come at once.'

When Reed was in conversation with one of the oldest Congressmen in the House and he asked him to what he attributed his long life, the elderly politician replied: 'I always have a slug of liquor every afternoon and I vote a straight Democratic ticket.' Reed, who was a teetotaller as well as being a fervent Republican, replied: 'Well that explains it – one poison offsets the other.'

Commenting on President Theodore Roosevelt he said: 'If there is one thing more than any other for which I admire him, it is his original discovery of the Ten Commandments.'

Of two fellow Congressmen for whom he did not have a high opinion he said: 'They can never open their mouths without subtracting from the sum total of human knowledge.'

And, on a member of the opposition, he said: 'The volume of his voice is equalled only by the volume of what he does not know.'

When William Springer, a Democrat, rose to his feet to ask for permission to make an apology for an incorrect attack he'd made on the Republican Party Reed exclaimed: 'No correction is needed – the House didn't believe you in the first place.'

On another occasion Congressman Jerry Lewis, who was rather good looking, raised a point of personal privilege when a tabloid newspaper referred to him as 'a thing of beauty and a joy forever'. Reed at first appeared to agree with him, saying it was a valid point, but then added: 'The newspaper should have said "a thing of beauty and a jaw forever".'

Commenting on the Senate: 'It is the little house – a close communion of old grannies and tabby cats. A place where good representatives go when they die.'

His view of those who specialize too much: 'If a man studies finance intimately, and continues his study long enough, it disqualifies him from talking intelligently upon any other subject. If he continues his studies still longer, it eventually disqualifies him from talking intelligently upon that!'

When Reed was campaigning in Maine during one presidential contest, a Democrat sat in the front row to heckle him. The Democrat kept asking impertinent and rude questions which Reed answered courteously.

It soon became obvious that the Democrat wanted to goad Reed into losing his temper, but Reed kept his cool. Finally, realizing that his ruse was not working, after a particularly polite and detailed answer to one of his questions, the heckler bawled: 'Oh, go to hell.' Reed immediately responded: 'I have travelled in many parts of the State and have spoken at many meetings, but this is the first time I have received an invitation to the Democratic headquarters.'

Among the most memorable of Speaker Reed's sayings are the following:

'A statesman is a politician who is dead.'

'All the wisdom of the world consists of shouting with the majority.'

Church minister Edward Hale became chaplain of the Senate in 1903. After he had been opening their sessions with a prayer for several weeks, a member of the public approached him in the street and said: 'Oh, I think I know you. Are you the man who prays for the Senators?'
'No,' Dr Hale snapped. 'I am the man who looks at the Senators and prays for the country.'

When North Carolina Senator Robert Strange was on his deathbed, he called for his son and said: 'On my tombstone I want the inscription "Here lies an honest Congressman".'
His son interjected: 'And then your name?'
'No,' said Strange, 'that won't be necessary. People who read it will say: "That's strange!" '

In 1919 President Wilson suffered a stroke. Senator Fall who had opposed some of Wilson's policies called to see him and said: 'Mr President, we have all been praying for you.' Wilson snapped: 'Ah, but which way?'

All good orators have an off day. Senator Robert La Follette from Wisconsin, usually an excellent speaker, was making a speech in February 1912 to the Periodical Publishers Association, and ignoring the late hour, he went on somewhat at length discussing the evils of corporate control of American newspapers. After he had been speaking for about an hour and a half on the same subject, he posed a rhetorical question to his audience: 'Is there a way out?' At which some wag got to his feet and shouted 'We hope so', and headed for the exit. Not only did this destroy the rest of La Follette's speech, but it effectively killed off his campaign for the Republican nomination for President that year.

Of course, not every time a member of the audience scores against the platform speaker is it intentional. At one political gathering Congressman Hancock of New York was due to address the audience at a meeting which started with some band music. After the orchestra had played a couple of numbers the chairman inadvertently insulted the guest speaker by asking: 'Do you want to speak now, or shall we let the audience enjoy themselves a little longer?'

Senator Claude Swanson of Virginia *was* deliberately insulted by an old dear in the audience after he had made a long and rambling speech. 'I liked your speech fine, Senator,' she said but then added, 'but it seems to me you missed several excellent opportunities.' The Senator was puzzled. 'Several opportunities for what?' he inquired. 'To quit,' she snapped.

Louisiana Senator Huey Long, elected in 1930, was regarded as a formidable opponent. He compared Herbert Hoover to a 'hoot owl' and Franklin D. Roosevelt to a 'scrootch owl'. Explaining himself, he said: 'A hoot owl bangs into the nest and knocks the hen clean off and catches her while she's falling. But a scrootch owl slips into the roost and scrootches up to the hen and talks softly to her. And then the hen just falls in love with him and the next thing you know, there ain't no hen.'

His name, Long, suited him. In 1935 he filibustered non-stop for fifteen and a half hours – one of the longest political speeches ever – against FDR's New Deal Bill. During the course of his speech he read to the Senate the complete Constitution of the United States, which caused satirist Will Rogers to quip: 'Most of the Senators thought he was reviewing a new book.'

He hit the nail on the head when talking about effective political tactics: 'In a political fight, if there is nothing in favour of your own side, start a row in the opposition camp.'

Long aroused the ire of Senator Glass who, after one of Long's speeches, announced that Long's electorate had outdone Caligula. 'Where Caligula made his horse a consul, Long's constituents have made the posterior of a horse a US Senator.'

Were he alive today, he would probably have been frequently suspended from the chamber for his bad language. With hindsight Long would probably have welcomed this to the alternative: on 8 September 1935, after making a particularly vicious speech, he was shot as he left the chamber. He died two days later.

William H. Taft, upon losing the presidential race to Woodrow Wilson, made the best fist of, for him, an appalling result, by quipping: 'I have one consolation. No candidate was elected ex-President by such a large majority.'

Anonymous on President Harry S. Truman: 'Among President Truman's many weaknesses was his utter inability to discriminate between history and histrionics.'

Theodore Roosevelt, who became President just after the turn of the century, was a master of the political barb. He once called President Castro of Venezuela 'an unspeakably villainous little monkey'.

Of an American judge: 'He is an amiable old fuzzy-wuzzy with sweetbread brains.'

On politician John Tyler: 'He's been called a mediocre man – but this is unwarranted flattery. He was a politician of monumental littleness.'

And he said of his successor Woodrow Wilson: 'He is a Byzantine logothete.'

On some demonstrators campaigning against blood sports: 'They are logical vegetarians of the flabbiest Hindoo type.'

Of William Jennings Bryan, he said: 'He represents that type of farmer whose gate hangs on one hinge, whose old hat supplies the place of the missing window pane and who is more likely to be found at the crossroad grocery store than behind the plough.'

Roosevelt was also responsible for a number of new phrases entering the vocabulary. Among his many utterances, he coined the sayings: 'the lunatic fringe', 'weazel words' and 'pussyfooting'.

Franklin D. Roosevelt said of his own career: 'I ask you to judge me by the enemies I have made.'

Texas Representative Sam Rayburn became Speaker of the

House of Representatives in 1940. He prided himself in telling the truth as he saw it, even if this meant upsetting his friends. His local preacher criticized Rayburn's support for President Truman's sacking of General MacArthur and added: 'If your constituents elect you to office again, they will be deaf, dumb and ignorant.' Rayburn turned to the preacher and said 'Being a believer in God and his word, which was "and on earth, peace and goodwill to all men", I fear that your conduct will not be conducive to carrying out these things. In other words, God travelling with you would be in poor company,' and then he walked off.

He snapped back at a critic who didn't think he was being partisan enough: 'Remember, number one: we're Americans first and Democrats second. And number two: we're builders not obstructionists. Any jackass can kick down the barn door, but it takes a carpenter to build one.'

And taking a swipe at a colleague who criticized the United States overseas: 'Politics should stop at the water's edge – when it comes to foreign policy you support your country.'

Among his many quips, insults and sayings the following are the best:

'Any man who becomes conceited and arrogant isn't big enough for the job.'

'Anyone who will cheat for you, will cheat against you.'

'There is a time to fish and a time to mend nets.'

'If there is anything I hate more than an old fogey, it's a young fogey.'

'No one has a finer command of language than the person who keeps his mouth shut.'

'Always tell the truth, then you'll never have to remember what you said the last time.'

Pat Harrison, a Mississippi Senator, did not have much time for Theodore Bilbo, a Senator from the same state, of whom he said: 'When Bilbo dies the epitaph on his gravestone should read: "Here lies Bilbo, deep in the dirt he loved so well."'

Once when John Allen of Mississippi was standing for Congress, he agreed to debate with his opponent, one W. B. Walker. Walker spoke first and said to the audience: 'Ladies and gentlemen, I want you to notice my opponent, Mr Allen. Just look at him sitting over there, big and fat. He's literally pregnant on other people's money, he has been in Congress so long.' When Allen's time came to speak, he patted his large stomach and said: 'What Mr Walker said is true about me being pregnant. If it's a girl I will name it Martha Washington. If it's a boy, I will name it George Washington, and if it's a jackass, I will name it W. B. Walker.'

For all candidates, most election campaigns have their difficulties. The reason is simple. It is impossible for a politician to express his opinion on the issues of the day without alienating some of his voters. The most successful constituency members are those who never talk politics in their own area, but confine themselves to issues where there is a broad consensus – such as improving the road network in the area, having the pavements resurfaced or, perhaps, campaigning for increased pensions. However, the general election public meeting is one occasion when a politician cannot avoid controversy, quite simply because he is certain to be asked a question on a current contentious issue. Texas Senator Tom Connally had a deft way of deflecting these questions. Once when he was in east Texas he was addressing an open-air crowd and his speech went down quite well. He was then asked a question by a farmer in the audience who said: 'How do you stand on the cotton issue?' Without a moment's hesitation Connally replied: 'I am OK on that one. Are there any other questions?'

President Calvin Coolidge effectively pleaded the cause for political inaction when he said: 'In politics, if you see ten troubles coming down the road, you can be sure that nine of them will run into the ditch before they reach you.'

During a rambling and almost incoherent speech made by a colleague in the Senate, Senator Eugene Millikin interrupted with: 'If the distinguished Senator will allow me, I will try to extricate him from his thoughts.'

Taking the blame for an unfortunate decision by a subordinate, President Harry S. Truman coined the phrase: 'The buck stops here.'

On trying to control children: 'I have found that the best way to give advice to your children, is to find out what they want and then advise them to do it.'

On himself: 'I am not sure that I managed it, but I did learn that a great leader is a man who has the ability to get other people to do what they don't want to do - and like it.'

And: 'Well, my speech seems to have been a hit according to all the newspapers. It shows you never can tell. I thought it was rotten.'

Slapping down a journalist who was commenting about Truman's poor family background: 'My father was not a failure. After all, he was the father of a President of the United States.'

To another journalist he barked: 'If you want to ask me an impudent question, that's all right. I will give you an impudent answer.'

On Richard Nixon's first attempt to become President: 'You don't send a fox to watch the chickens just because he has had a lot of experience in the hen house.'

Towards the end of the war he said: 'If we see that Germany is winning the war, we ought to help Russia, and if Russia is winning, we ought to help Germany, and in that way let them kill as many as possible.'

Truman commenting on his successor: 'Some of the newspapers are making snide remarks about Mrs Eisenhower saying she has a drinking problem. It wouldn't surprise me if she did because look what that poor woman has to put up with. She's married to a no-good son of a bitch.'

Accurately summing up the loneliness of the world's most powerful job, he quipped: 'If you really want a friend in Washington, get a dog.'

Famous American cartoonist Al Capp, who created the character Li'l Abner, was attending a party when he was introduced by the hostess to President Truman. 'Mr President, I'd like you to meet the famous comic strip cartoonist, Al Capp,' to which the President inquired: 'Which comic strip?' The hostess turned to Mr Capp and said to him: 'I'd like to introduce you to President Truman,' to which Capp quipped back: 'Which country?'

Among his other comments, the following are worthy of note:

'Don't talk about rope in the house of somebody who has been hanged.'

'Whenever an elector tells me he's non-partisan, I know that he's going to vote against me.'

'Statesmen are more expendable than soldiers.'

Failed presidential candidate Adlai Stevenson was a great wit, but suffered from the fact that he was not 'televisual'. In some respects, as a presidential candidate he was the complete opposite of Ronald Reagan. Although his televised interviews made a poor impression, he had a sharp and crackling wit and was not afraid to speak his mind.

The following are among his most memorable quotes:

'A lie is an abomination unto the Lord – and a very pleasant help in time of trouble.'

'A hungry man is not a free man.'

'A free society is one where it is safe to be unpopular.'

'Flattery is all right – if you don't inhale.'

'The human race has improved everything except the human race.'

And adapting the saying by Lord Acton ('Power tends to corrupt and absolute power corrupts absolutely'), he said: 'Power corrupts, but lack of power corrupts absolutely.'

Another failed presidential candidate Barry Goldwater was regarded by the majority of Americans as unelectable because of his extremist views. However, he did have the ability to encapsulate his arguments succinctly. He said: 'Minority groups now speak much more loudly than do majority groups which I classify as the forgotten American . . . the man who pays his taxes, prays, behaves himself, stays out of trouble and works for his government.'

During the early 1960s the Republican Goldwater often came into confrontation with Liberal Senator Hubert Humphrey. With some justification Humphrey regarded Goldwater as extremely right-wing and reactionary. When they met at a reception given in Hollywood for a movie company, Humphrey said: 'Senator Goldwater would have been a great success in the movies – working for Eighteenth Century-Fox.'

Goldwater, however, soon got his own back. Of Humphrey he remarked: 'He talks so fast that listening to him is like trying to read *Playboy* with your wife turning the pages.'

Tired of being attacked as an 'extremist' by his opponents, who had claimed to be 'moderates', he said: 'May I remind you that extremism in the defence of liberty is no vice. And let me tell you that moderation in the pursuit of justice is not a virtue.'

Of Democratic President Lyndon B. Johnson he snapped: 'He fiddled while Detroit burned and he faddled while men died [in Vietnam].'

On state interference and 'big government': 'A government that is big enough to give you all you want, is big enough to take it all away.'

Hubert Humphrey is perhaps better remembered not as a Senator but as a failed presidential candidate. After his ambitions to enter the White House had been destroyed, he gave some good advice to losers: 'If you can't cry a bit in politics, the only other thing you'll have is hate.'

Humphrey acknowledged that he was often long-winded, remarking to one colleague: 'I can't even clear my throat in less than three minutes.'

Governor George Wallace often gave the impression that he thrived on hate. When asked by the press how he would react to demonstrators blocking his way he snapped back: 'If any demonstrator lies down in front of my car – it will be the last car he will ever lie down in front of.'

President John F. Kennedy may have been right when he claimed: 'Mothers all want their sons to grow up to be President – but they don't want them to become politicians in the process.'

And JFK on Senator Everett Dirksen: 'The Wizard of Ooze.'

Robert Jackson accurately summed up one of the problems of a democracy: 'The price of freedom of religion or of speech or of the press is that we must put up with, and even pay for, a good deal of rubbish.'

Former Democratic President Lyndon Johnson did not think much of Jack Kennedy before Kennedy became President, saying of him: 'He's just a flash in the pan. The boy has no record of substance.'

And of former Kennedy aide Bob Griffin he thought even less: 'He's not going anywhere. That elongated son of a bitch looks down his nose at me like I'm shit. Every time I see him I almost go through the roof.'

In 1948 before Johnson had aspirations to become President, he stood for election to the Senate. He won, but by such a narrow margin that some of his opponents alleged that he had rigged the ballot. They referred to him sarcastically as 'Landslide Lyndon'.

These allegations led some Republicans to tell the story of a man who came across a small Mexican boy who was crying his heart out. 'Why are you crying?' asked the man. The Mexican lad replied, 'My daddy doesn't love me.' The man was rather amazed by this response as he knew the boy's father had been dead for some time. 'But your daddy is dead,' the man replied. 'Yes, cried the lad, 'but he came back to vote for Lyndon Johnson and didn't come to see me.'

Johnson was a ruthless politician. Before he became President, he ran into difficulties when fighting a primary election. It was in a state that was distant from his home and where he was not well known and he was fighting against a worthy opponent who was a church-going, respected pillar of society. Johnson, who was not making much impact, discussed with his campaign manager what he should do. During the meeting, Johnson suggested that they should leak the news to the press that their distinguished opponent had been guilty of vile sexual practices. His team were aghast and unanimous that it should not be done. 'It's not true,' an aide protested. 'No,' said Johnson, 'it's not, but I just want to hear him deny it.'

Of Republican President Gerald Ford, Johnson remarked: 'He

is a nice guy, but he played too much football with his helmet off.'

His advice on when to trust colleagues: 'I never trust a man unless I've got his pecker in my pocket.'

Johnson had a simple view of what life was like in the Oval Office: 'Being President is like being a jackass in a hailstorm. There's nothing to do but stand there and take it.'

On a speech by Republican Richard Nixon: 'I may not know much but I know chicken shit from chicken salad.'

His definition of foreigners: 'They ain't like the folk you were reared with.'

On conquest: 'The best fertilizer for a piece of land is the footprints of its owner.'

James Michael Curley, four times Mayor of Boston, was something of a rascal who didn't mind bending the rules to get his own way. Hit motto used to be: 'Do unto others as they wish to do unto you – but do it first.' One opponent whom Curley did it to first started to refer to him as 'old cabbage ears', and the name stuck.

His methods were unorthodox, but usually effective. Once when his office was owed a large amount of money, he realized that he was unable to pay all of the city employees on time. He personally telephoned the chairman of the company who owed the debt and said: 'I have a nice picture of you at home and a nice picture of the beautiful house you have in the country. If I don't get the money for my payroll by this evening, I am going to print both these pictures in the local newspaper. Under your picture it will say: "This is the man who is responsible for city employees not being paid" and under the picture of your house it will say: "And this is where he lives." ' He then put down the phone. The ruse worked and Curley got his money on time.

His view of 'Tip' O'Neill was extremely basic: 'He's a fat bastard.'

When Senator Robert Kennedy was standing in the Democratic presidential primaries in 1968 he was due to address a meeting of farmers. He arrived rather early and walked in to the back of the room, where he was unnoticed at first. He overheard some of the farmers grumbling about what a drain it would be on the budget 'if those nine or ten Kennedy children get into the White House'. Announcing his arrival, he then added: 'Yes, I've got ten kids and they all drink milk. Tell me anyone else who is doing that much for the farmer.'

Kennedy also quipped: 'One fifth of the people are against everything all the time.'

Senator Eugene McCarthy on being a successful politician: 'It is like being a football coach. You have to be smart enough to understand the game and dumb enough to think it's important.'

Former President Richard Nixon was always a controversial figure. On politics he remarked: 'There is one thing solid and fundamental in politics – the law of change. What's "up" today is "down" tomorrow.'

His advice to young politicians: 'Always remember others

may hate you but those who hate you don't win unless you hate them. And then you destroy yourself.'

His maxim for political success: 'To be popular in office, you need an enemy. Reagan had the USSR and Congress. Clinton, as yet, has not found one.'

This thumb-nail assessment of President Boris Yeltsin has yet to be bettered. 'He burns all his candles at both ends and he is compulsive. I give him only slightly more than a 50 per cent chance of success. But he's got guts.'

To an aide: 'Use all the rhetoric, so long as it doesn't cost money.'

And: 'Voters quickly forget what a man says.'

Harry Truman disliked Nixon, calling him a 'no-good lying bastard.' Adding for good measure: 'He can lie out of both sides of his mouth at the same time, and even if he caught himself telling the truth, he'd lie just to keep his hand in.'

Despite a landslide re-election victory Nixon never completed his second term, being forced to resign in disgrace following the Watergate hearings. Shortly before his death, showing that he still had a sense of humour, he said: 'I hear that whenever anyone in the White House tells a lie, I get a royalty.'

Giving his views on political speeches, Nixon opined: 'I have often said that the best political speech is poetry. Jesse Jackson is a poet but Michael Dukakis* is a word-processor.'

Anonymous on Nixon: 'He's the kind of guy who would call in phoney reprieves to Death Row.'

American car sticker in 1960, when J. F. Kennedy was the

* Democratic presidential contender in 1988 who lost to George Bush.

Democratic candidate and Richard Nixon was standing for the Republicans: 'Thank God only one of them can win!'

At the time of Nixon's troubles over Watergate, seen in graffiti on a wall in Washington was: 'Where is Lee Harvey Oswald now that his country needs him?'*

Nixon's view of his predecessor: 'People said that my language was bad, but Jesus, you should have heard LBJ.'

Anonymous on Nixon: 'Nixon impeached himself – he gave us Ford as his revenge.'

Nixon silencing a heckler: 'The jaw-bone of an ass is just as dangerous a weapon today as in Samson's time.'

Anonymous on Nixon: 'Nixon has one simple political principle: if two wrongs don't make a right – try a third,' and: 'Nixon told us he was going to take crime off the streets. He did. He took it into the White House.'

Among Nixon's best quips are the following:

'Never strike a king unless you kill him. In politics you shouldn't hit your opponent unless you knock him out.'

'A good politician knows not only how to count votes but how to make his vote count.'

Many felt that Richard Nixon should have heeded the words of John G. Diefenbaker, former Prime Minister of Canada, who said: 'Freedom is the right to be wrong, not the right to do wrong.'

---

* President Kennedy's assassin.

During the term of office of President Nixon, a Republican Senator wanted Congress to appropriate $600 million to help bring the nation's sewage disposal system up to date. He knew that President Nixon was opposed to the measure and, therefore, he prepared a well-argued and detailed speech on the subject, in which he discussed household effluent and the waste-disposal systems in some detail.

When he finished his address, New Hampshire Senator Norris Cotton approached him and said: 'I never realized until now what you're an expert on, but now I know.' 'What's that, Norris?' asked the Senator. Cotton responded tersely: 'Shit.' The Senator was nonplussed for a moment and then recovered the situation with his response: 'Norris, can you think of anything more important to be an expert on in the Senate than that?'

Former President Gerald Ford was frequently ridiculed in satire shows for his clumsiness. However, occasionally he put his detractors in their place. He once said: 'A bronco is something that kicks and bucks, twists and turns, and very seldom goes in one direction. We have one of those things here in Washington – it's called the Congress.'

One story told in Washington was that when President Ford was due to take a trip on Air Force One, he couldn't remember the number of the flight.

It was also said of him: 'Gerald Ford was unknown throughout America until he became President. Now he's unknown throughout the world.'

Ford was not, however, without wit himself. He once said of Senator and presidential hopeful Hubert Humphrey: 'I can still remember the first time I ever heard him speak. He was in the second hour of a five-minute talk.'

Ford served in Congress before achieving his country's highest office. Once, when Hubert Humphrey was making a lengthy speech, Ford, who had just entered the chamber, asked his neighbour: 'What follows Humphrey?' He received the riposte: 'Christmas.'

In 1973 beef prices in America were soaring. In order to try to protect the consumer, Congressman Frank Anions from Chicago introduced an amendment in committee to freeze the price of beef. Somewhat to his surprise the amendment was passed.

Afterwards he was interviewed by the *Wall Street Journal* and he expressed his pleasure at the successful amendment adding, 'This is a victory for the American people.'

However, as is often the case in politics, his victory was short-lived. Overnight, beef farmers went into action and started lobbying politicians. They were so successful that the next day the committee voted to reconsider Anions's amendment and decided to reject it.

The same reporter from the *Wall Street Journal* sought out the Chicago Congressman and asked him again for his reaction now that his amendment had been rejected. Rather tersely Anions stated: 'The American people got fucked.' The shocked reporter protested: 'I can't use that quote – this is a family newspaper.' Turning to leave, Anions snapped: 'In that case, tell them the American *family* got fucked,' and walked off.

And on that subject, Mrs Lillian Carter, the mother of former President Jimmy surprised even the liberal press when she said: 'Sometimes when I look at my children, I say to myself "Lillian, you should have stayed a virgin."'

The use of the insult during an election campaign can backfire, particularly if the public perceive that the gibe is unfair or just downright nasty. Governor Pat Brown of California, when challenged at the polls by Ronald Reagan, ran a series of insulting television adverts that opened with the line: 'I am running against an actor . . . and you know who killed Abraham Lincoln, don't you?' This backfired badly and Reagan won the subsequent election by a landslide.

Reagan's more restrained retort to Pat Brown was: 'He is one of those liberals* who thinks that all the world's problems can be solved by throwing taxpayers' money at them.'

Ronald Reagan was known as 'The Great Communicator' due to his consummate skill on television, and also, on Capitol Hill, as 'The Great Persuader' because of his ability to persuade a number of Democrats, who controlled Congress, to agree to his programme. Despite the fact that he never had a majority in the House, Reagan managed to push through most of his manifesto by splitting the opposition.

His popularity was – and is – undoubtedly due to the fact that he came over on television as 'a nice guy', someone totally free of malice. However, when he thought the occasion demanded it, he was not afraid to use invective to make his point. Before the collapse of Communism he caused

---

* The word 'liberal' has a different connotation in USA politics to its UK meaning. Reagan was being derogatory. Our equivalent description would be 'left-winger.'

a furore when he referred to the USSR as 'the evil empire'. Liberal opinion was similarly outraged in 1986 when he referred to Iran as 'Murder Incorporated'.

His view of Colonel Gaddafi's regime in Libya was similarly robust: 'We are not going to tolerate these attacks from states run by the strangest collection of misfits, loony tunes and squalid criminals since the advent of the Third Reich.' He later said of Gaddafi: 'Not only a barbarian but flaky.'

During his time as Governor of California, Reagan was faced with a delegation of students who took over his office. Some were barefooted, several were wearing torn T-shirts, and when the Governor entered the room, no one stood up. The ringleader said to Reagan: 'We want to talk to you but we think it's impossible for you to understand us. You weren't raised in a time of instant communications or satellites and computers, solving problems in seconds. We now live in an age of space travel and journeys to the moon, of jet travel and high-speed electronics. You didn't have those things when you were young . . .' At this point Reagan interrupted the student spokesman and said: 'No, we didn't have those things when we were your age – we invented them.' Not only did Reagan silence the students, but he let it be known that his only policy would be that they should 'Obey the rules or get out.'

Just before he became President, Reagan made a devastating attack on his predecessor, telling a crowd: 'A depression is when you're out of work. A recession is when your neighbour is out of work. And a recovery is when Jimmy Carter is out of work.'

During his presidency Reagan maintained his friendships with the world of showbusiness. Once, at a White House banquet, he found himself talking to old friend Bob Hope, a golf fanatic. Hope inquired whether Reagan had any time for golf and asked the President: 'What's your handicap?' Reagan shot back: 'Congress.'

Commenting on former Speaker of the House 'Tip' O'Neill, Reagan said: 'He could be sincere and friendly when he wanted to be, but he could also turn off his charm and friendship like a light-switch and become as bloodthirsty as a piranha.'

On his former Secretary of State Alexander Haig: 'He could pound the table and seemed ready to explode. He was insecure. I thought he was seeing shadows in a mirror.'

During the 1984 presidential race, when Reagan was seeking re-election, his opponent Walter Mondale quipped: 'I don't like to attack Ronald Reagan as being too old for the job, but I remember that in his first movie Gabby Hayes got the girl.'

These quips about Reagan's age backfired however. During the televised presidential debate, a journalist asked Reagan outright: 'Will age be an issue in this election?' Reagan gently replied: 'I am not prepared, for party political advantage, to make reference to the *youth* and *inexperience* of my opponent.' Even his rival, Mondale, could not help laughing at this response and from then on the 'age' issue was never mentioned again in the campaign.

During his period as President and before the Berlin Wall was pulled down, one of Reagan's favourite stories was of Leonid Brezhnev on his deathbed giving advice to his successor Yuri Andropov. Raising himself on one arm Brezhnev said: 'Let me give you one piece of advice. When you take over from me, make sure in whatever you do that the Soviet people follow you.' At which point Andropov replied to the dying Brezhnev: 'Don't worry. If they don't follow me, I'll make sure that they follow you.'

Reagan's description of the USSR before the Berlin Wall came down: 'I think at last President Gorbachev realized he was head of an economic basket case.'

In the 1988 American presidential race, answering a journalist's reference to his young age for such high office, Dan Quayle, then candidate for the vice-presidency, pointed out that John Kennedy was of a similar age when he stood for the presidency. This led the Democratic vice-presidential candidate Lloyd Bentsen to say: 'I knew President Kennedy and Senator you're no Jack Kennedy.' The insult hurt but it was not until four years later that a Republican politician turned the insult back upon the Democrats. On the opening day of the Republican convention in 1992, Reagan referred to Bill Clinton's claim that he was the new Thomas Jefferson, and added: 'I knew Thomas Jefferson. He was a friend of mine – and Governor Clinton, you ain't no Thomas Jefferson.'

Early in his presidency even his opponents were impressed by Reagan's first televised budget speech, in which he used a handful of small change to illustrate the effects of inflation on the value of the dollar. A Democratic rival observed: 'Carter would have emphasized all the wrong words. Ford would have fumbled and dropped the cash – and Nixon would have pocketed it.'

On the problems he faced in office, Reagan said: 'In this present crisis government is not the solution to our problems. Government is the problem.'

And on his political opponents: 'The leaders of the Democratic Party have gone so far left, they've left the country.'

After Bill Clinton had admitted that he smoked pot while a student but claimed he had not inhaled, Reagan gave some advice to his supporters on the Democratic candidate's election promises: 'When you hear all of that smoky rhetoric billowing out of Clinton's headquarters, take the advice of their nominee – don't inhale.'

Reagan's view of government: 'Governments tend not to solve problems, only rearrange them.'

Disarming his critics, during one of his last public speeches, he opened his remarks with the comment: 'I am delighted to be here. Tonight is, of course, a very special evening for me. Mind you, at my age, *every* evening is special.'

On his own career. 'It's been the honour of my life to be President. It's been quite a journey and I have had my share of victories. The thing about being born in 1911 is that in my lifetime I have seen the birth of Communism and the death of Communism. Today we still need to remember that freedom is fragile.'

Explaining his successful campaigning methods, Reagan revealed his strategy: 'I always campaign as if I am one vote behind.'

And his view of the USA: 'All great change in America begins at the dinner table.'

Former Labour minister Denis (now Lord) Healey was not impressed with Reagan's economic record, saying: 'He has done for monetarism what the Boston Strangler did for door-to-door salesmen.'

And the views of veteran Republican Barry Goldwater on the former actor-President: 'He can't decide whether he was born in a log cabin or a manger.'

Former President George Bush had a vicious line on his Democratic opponent during the 1992 election: 'I consulted with John Major and other leaders on foreign policy issues – Bill Clinton takes advice from Boy George.'

In a similar vein, again on Clinton: 'While I bit the bullet, he bit his nails. His policy can be summed on by a road sign he's probably seen, "slippery when wet". He says he's for one thing and then comes out for another. He's like that on a lot of issues – first one side then the other. He's been spotted in more places than Elvis Presley.'

Bush had a neat line in 1988 during his first election campaign. He said: 'My opponent has a problem. He won't get elected unless things get worse – and things won't get worse unless he gets elected.'

Bush on Andrew Young: 'He is a loose cannon on a rolling deck.'

On Clinton's policies: 'He says he wants to tax the rich, but he defines rich as anyone who has a job. You've heard of the separation of powers. Well Bill Clinton practises a different theory – the power of separations. His government would have the power to separate you from your wallet.'

And returning to his Presley theme: 'Clinton's plan for America really is "Elvis economics" – 'the country will be checking into the Heartbreak Hotel!'

On talking to the press: 'Never answer a hypothetical question – it gets you to beyond where you want to be.'

During the 1992 presidential election, Bush called the Democratic team 'a couple of bozos', which led to the retort from President Clinton: 'All I can say is a bozo makes people laugh and Bush makes people cry . . . and America is going to be laughing on election night.'

His comments before polling day on the way the Clinton campaign was conducted could with hindsight be applied to his own performance. He unwisely remarked: 'It reminds me of the old conman's advice to the new kid when he said, "Son, if you're being run out of town, just get in front and make it look like a parade."'

The penchant of a free press to exaggerate bad news is well-known. Lord Tombs, former Rolls-Royce boss, once startled a group of reporters by announcing: 'Gentlemen, I have a problem for you. We have just won a massive order which secures hundreds of jobs. As I therefore have only *good* news to announce, you won't have a typeface small enough for the story.'

After months of gloomy news reports, just before his failed re-election bid Bush, in a similar vein, remarked: 'When the Berlin Wall fell, I half expected to see a headline "Wall falls, three border guards lose jobs."'

A critic has recently said of former President Bush: 'All hat and no cattle.'

Former vice-president Dan Quayle has long been the butt-end of press criticism and political sniping from the Democrats. During the early stages of the 1992 presidential election he gave his detractors ammunition by mis-spelling potato as 'potatoe'. This led to howls of derision which Quayle turned back against the Democrats by quipping: 'If Bill Clinton is a moderate, then I am a world-champion speller.'

Over the years, Quayle has continued to give his opponents much grist to the mill merely by his *own* utterances, which have all but destroyed his credibility as a heavyweight politician. 'If we don't succeed, we run the risk of failure' he once famously opined. So far has his reputation sunk that the announcement by this former Vice President in 1999 that he was 'thinking' of running for President at the next election was greeted with incredulity by many.

You only have to reflect on some of his other utterances, listed below, to see why his reputation has suffered so badly:

'I was recently on a tour of Latin America and the only regret I have was that I didn't study Latin harder in school so I could converse with those people.'

'I stand by all the misstatements that I've made.'

'We are ready for any unforeseen event that may or may not occur.'

'I love California, I practically grew up in Phoenix.'

'What a waste it is to lose one's mind. Or not to have a mind is being very wasteful. How true that is.'

'Republicans understand the importance of bondage between a mother and child.'

'It's time for the human race to enter the solar system.'

Thomas 'Tip' O'Neill, former Democratic Speaker of the House of Representatives, was for many years one of America's most colourful public figures. He retired in 1986 having served for thirty-four years as a member of Congress, ten of those as Speaker – the longest continuous term in the United States.

On John F. Kennedy: 'The first time I met Jack Kennedy I couldn't believe this skinny pasty-looking kid was a candidate for anything. He had absolutely no political experience. Although he was a Democrat, looking back I'd say he was only nominally a Democrat. He was a Kennedy, which was more than a family affiliation. It quickly developed into an entire political party. He certainly knew how to charm the ladies and he always made a point of appealing to what he called "womanpower" – the untapped resource.'

On Bobby Kennedy: 'He was a self-important upstart and a know-it-all. Jack Kennedy had not grown up in the school of hard knocks. He was used to people loving him and if someone said something mean about him and it got back to him, he would wonder why they didn't like him. But with Bobby ... when Bobby hated you, you stayed hated.'

On former Congressman Howard Smith of Virginia: 'A taciturn, arrogant son of a bitch who was no more a Democrat than the man in the moon. As far as he was concerned, the civil war was still going on.'

On former President Lyndon Johnson: 'As a professional politician he had the right idea but he was crude about it. His political style was overwhelming and there was nothing subtle about it.'

And his view of the Kennedy-Johnson relationship: 'The vice-presidency is never an easy office to occupy but it rankled Johnson that this young, rich upstart was in the White House while he, who had come up the hard way, was the all-but-forgotten number two man.'

O'Neill's comments on former presidential hopeful Eugene McCarthy: 'He was a whimsical fellow with a meanness in his heart. He was lazy and a bit of a dreamer. He had the support of all the way-out flaky liberals in the country.'

On Wayne Hayes, a former Congressman: 'He was an excellent orator but had a mean streak and was often abusive to people he didn't agree with. Even when he praised you he did it with a nasty twist. When he resigned from Congress most of us were delighted to see him go.'

O'Neill's view of the American news reporting team of Evans and Novak: 'They ought to be called "Errors and Nofacts".'

On politics: 'Power is never given – it is only taken.'

On former President Richard Nixon: 'He was brilliant but he had a quirk in his personality that made him suspicious of everybody – including members of his own cabinet. He was a leery and nervous President.'

On former President Gerald Ford: 'Although he was wrong most of the time, he was decently wrong.'

On former presidential hopeful George McGovern: 'His nomination was a disaster. He never should have been selected as the Democratic candidate but he was chosen by the cast of *Hair*. I was absolutely shocked when the young people in the party picked him as their champion. The party has an occasional suicidal tendency and you didn't need to be a pollster like Harris to see that McGovern was going to get creamed. In the eyes of many Americans, George McGovern was so far to the left he was off the map.'

On former President Jimmy Carter: 'He came in young and vigorous but left a tired man. When it came to the politics of Washington, he never really understood how the system worked – he didn't want to learn about it either. He rode into town like a knight on a white horse, but while the gentleman leading the charge was capable, too many of the troops he brought with him were amateurs. But that didn't prevent them from being arrogant. Too many of his aides – especially his chief of staff Hamilton Jordan – came to Washington with a chip on their shoulder and never changed. Those guys came in like a bunch of jerks and went out the same way.'

And warming to his main target, Mr Jordan: 'He is a son of a bitch. As far as he is concerned, the House Speaker is someone you bought on sale at Radio shack. I prefer to call him Hannibal Jerken.'

When O'Neill became Speaker of the House of Representatives, a young Congressman asked him why he was not being included in the decision-making. O'Neill shot back: 'Although I take you seriously, you must remember that when a storm comes along, I don't want to grab on to a young sapling that sways in the wind. In difficult times, I prefer to go along with the sturdy old oak.'

His view on the difference between the two houses in the US Congress: 'Congressmen are the workhorses while the Senators are the show horses.'

On political lobbying: 'I believe that public protest is more effective than a silent majority. I am convinced that the squeaky wheel gets the grease.'

And expanding his views on the subject: 'When someone asks me why the Greeks in America always get a hearing for their side, and the Turks can't get anywhere, I will say: "That's because nobody knows a Turk, but everybody knows the people who run all those restaurants." It's the same with the Arab-Israeli conflict. The experts can come up with a dozen reasons to explain why America supports Israel, usually that Israel is the only true democracy in the Middle East or that the Soviet Union used to provide huge arms shipments to Israel's enemies. That might be true enough, but to the average American it often boils down to something more basic – the fact that some of his friends and neighbours happen to be Jewish. The answer is simple. All politics is local.'

On the office of President: 'What Jimmy Carter failed to understand is that the American people want a magisterial air in the White House which explains why the Kennedys and the Reagans were far more popular than the Carters and the Lyndon Johnsons – most people prefer a little pomp in their Presidents.'

On former President Ronald Reagan: 'The press saw Lyndon Johnson as crude, Richard Nixon as a liar, Gerald Ford as a bumbler, Jimmy Carter as incompetent, but they were certainly rooting for Ronald Reagan. Reagan has enormous personal appeal and he quickly became a folk hero. He performed so beautifully on the tube that he could sell anything, but he has been a rich man's President. He has shown no care or compassion for the poor, but when it comes to giving money to the Pentagon or tax breaks to the wealthy, Reagan has a heart of gold. He is Herbert Hoover with a smile. He is a cheerleader for selfishness.'

Continuing his attack on Reagan, he did concede the former President's strengths: 'In 1986 he started singing that familiar song that those Americans who were out of work could get jobs if they really wanted to. I couldn't believe he was still spouting this nonsense. This was Ronald Reagan at his worst, but later that same day I saw the President at his best. After our first meeting the space shuttle Challenger exploded after take-off and that evening the President went on television. He made a masterly speech and as I listened to him, I had a tear in my eye and a lump in my throat. Ronald Reagan may have lacked some of the management skills that a President needs, but he's the best public speaker ever and in this respect he dwarfs both Roosevelt and Kennedy.'

Getting his own back Reagan later commented on 'Tip' O'Neill (a man about the same height as Reagan but considerably larger in girth): 'I like to keep in shape by jogging three times a day around "Tip" O'Neill.'

A member of the public was not quite as tactful. When he saw O'Neill leaving a plane he buttonholed the Speaker and said: 'Leave the President alone, you fat bastard.'

Television can be deceptive. As Margaret Thatcher once said: 'Selective seeing is believing.' After Congress admitted television cameras, a number of representatives would take advantage of the 'Special Orders' procedure to attack their opponents. This is a part of the day in Congress which is similar to the adjournment debate in the British House of Commons. It is a period at the end of the day's business where any member is entitled to take the floor and to speak for up to an hour (in the House of Commons it is usually limited to thirty minutes) on any subject of his choosing. On most occasions the chamber is empty and Special Orders speeches are usually made for consumption back in the constituency. On one occasion Robert Walker, a Congressman from Pennsylvania, used his speech to attack another Congressman who he knew had left the building. He attacked his colleague's voting record and generally criticized him. Under the rules of Congress, the television camera was focused only on Walker, so anyone watching TV at home would assume that not only was the House full, but that also the politician being insulted was sitting, inert, just listening to the diatribe. To encourage this perception, Walker would pause from time to time as if to give his opponent the chance to reply. The inference drawn by the viewer was that the man being slagged off was actually accepting by his silence the criticism being levelled.

Walker might have got away with this, but for the fact that 'Tip' O'Neill, then House Speaker, was watching the performance from the television monitor in his office. O'Neill called the director of television and told him to pan the cameras around the entire chamber. He did so and the television viewer then saw that the chamber was empty. Walker's tactics, therefore, backfired badly, although he and his fellow Republicans did lodge a complaint against O'Neill for altering the rules of transmission. O'Neill had the last word by publicly rebuking Walker and his colleague, Congressman Gingrich, for attempting to deceive the public.

Among O'Neill's other comments the following are worthy of note:

'The press, in its cynical way, loves to portray just about every congressional trip as a junket.'

'Money is the mother's milk of politics.'

In 1988, Mark Russell said of former presidential hopeful Michael Dukakis: 'The one bland Greek in the world and he's running for President . . . Zorba the Clerk.'

Coleman Young, the Mayor of Detroit, recently said of politician-cum-preacher, Jesse Jackson: 'Jackson ain't never run nothing but that mouth of his.'

Former Congressman John Le Boutillier had a sharp tongue for nearly everyone. Commenting on Harvard University he said: 'The University is filled with hypocritical, bleeding-heart leftists.' At the time of his election in 1980 Le Boutillier, who was only twenty-seven, was the youngest member of congress, but that didn't stop him from insulting some senior politicians. He referred to President Carter as a 'complete bird-brain', Democrat presidential hopeful George McGovern was dismissed as 'scum', and he called Speaker 'Tip' O'Neill 'big, fat, and out of control – just like the Federal Government.'

He even went to the unusual lengths of campaigning against the Speaker's re-election using the slogan 'Repeal O'Neill.' Despite this O'Neill was comfortably re-elected.

Author Philip Stern caused a furore in 1998 with his book *The Best Congress Money Can Buy*. To attempt to make his point he put a one-dollar note inside 509 copies of his book and posted them to all members of Congress.

A few dollars were returned with a brief note from the Congressmen concerned saying that they could not accept cash, some Congressmen kept the money and the book, but Stern was surprised with the letter he received from Jerry Lewis, the Californian Republican representative who returned the dollar note wrapped in toilet paper. In an accompanying letter Lewis wrote: 'Anyone who presumes that people who seek to serve in public affairs can have their principles purchased by one dollar, or one thousand dollars, should look into a mirror and carefully measure their own character.'

Senator Jesse Helms went one better. He kept the dollar and wrote back: 'I don't resent your implication that Congress can be "bought" because I am willing to assume that you have some exceptions in mind and that I am one of the exceptions.'

A Mississippi Congressman, Robert Roberts, was once assailed by a constituent who complained that he took little part in debates in the House of Representatives while other Congressmen made many speeches and attracted a lot of national attention. Roberts took his constituent to task, replying: 'When I was a young man, I used to ride a horse and whenever I came to the bank of a stream, I put my ear to the ground and ascertained whether water made a noise. At that place, I always marched in – it was sure to be the shallowest place.' And with that he walked off.

The office of vice-president of the United States of America is perhaps the most maligned position in *any* democracy. Franklin D. Roosevelt said that the job was 'the spare tyre in the US government.'

Roosevelt's vice-president was John Nance Garner who said that 'A great man may be a vice-president, but he can't be a great vice-president because the office in itself is unimportant.'

President Kennedy summed up why the post can be an unrewarding one: 'The vice-presidency is the worst of both worlds. You don't have any power and the Secret Service is always on your tail.'

Lyndon Johnson had practical experience of the job. He was VP to Kennedy before becoming President himself following Kennedy's assassination. He thought even less of the number two job, saying that it 'wasn't worth a pitcher of warm piss.'

Earlier, John Adams, the first US vice-president, said: 'My country has in its wisdom contrived for me the most insignificant office that has ever been conceived by the imagination of man.'

Referring to the vice-president's duty of having to preside over sittings of the Senate, Adams continued: 'It is a punishment to have to hear other men talk five hours every day and not be at liberty to talk at all oneself.'

Harry Truman, who was Franklin D. Roosevelt's third vice-president, had a similar turn of phrase to Johnson. Being marginally less crude, he said of vice-presidents: 'They are about as useful as a cow's fifth teat.'

Roosevelt appeared to share these sentiments. Once, when a tinkling chandelier in the White House disturbed his slumbers, he ordered the staff to remove it. When he was asked what should be done with the offending item he said: 'Take it to the vice-president – he needs something to keep him awake.'

Walter Mondale, whose challenge for the presidency against Ronald Reagan ended in disaster, had earlier served as vice-president. He shared the views previously expressed about the office. He often told the story about a man who lived near Three Mile Island who had been assured by an expert that the area was safe from radioactivity 'because the President had visited the area.' When the man questioned this and asked: 'What makes you think that that proves it is safe?' he received the response: 'If it wasn't safe, they would have sent the vice-president.'

One US Congressman received a highly critical letter from a woman in his home town, who was upset by the way he had voted. In the course of her missive she said: 'Congressman, even if you were St Peter, because of what you have done, I would not vote for you.' The Congressman wrote back explaining the reasons for his vote and added at the end of his letter: 'I note your statement, that even if I were St Peter you wouldn't vote for me. Allow me to point out, however, that if I was St Peter, you couldn't vote for me. You wouldn't be in my district.'

Taking a swipe at education wets, Republican Representative John Ashbrook said: 'A Harvard professor is an educator who thinks that the American eagle has two left wings.'

In the United States political invective during an election is known as 'negative campaigning'. In America candidates are allowed to advertise on both radio and television and a recent survey revealed that almost 90 per cent of these adverts are 'negative'. Rather than extol the virtues of the candidate who is paying for the advert, it appears that it is more effective to rubbish one's opponent.

My favourite 'negative' ad was one used by an unknown candidate who was fighting an experienced and long-servicing incumbent in a state election. The incumbent, predictably ran a series of ads emphasizing his experience, adding that he had 'been serving in the Statehouse a long time' and was 'the voice of experience'.

The response to his challenger was devastating. Against a background shot of someone attempting to slice a golf ball, a voice-over said: 'Do you have an elderly uncle who likes playing golf? You know, he's been playing it for years. He is very experienced at the game. And yet he's just as bad now as when he first started! Well, it's the same over at the Statehouse.'

The challenger won the seat.

The former Senator for Ohio, Stephen Young, once received a letter saying: 'You are a stupid fool for favouring gun control. I am sure you could walk upright under a snake's tail with your hat on and have plenty of headroom.' The constituent also gave his address and telephone number and said: 'I would welcome the opportunity to have intercourse with you.'

Young rose to this insult and replied: 'Sir, I am in receipt of your most insulting letter, and I note your offer in the final paragraph where you welcome the opportunity of me having intercourse with you. No, indeed. You go ahead and have intercourse with yourself.'

Young also said to a local lawyer who insisted on giving him some advice as to how he should vote. 'Don't give me any more of this unsolicited advice. I know it costs nothing, but that is exactly what it's worth.'

Summing up his own philosophy he said: 'Sarcasm is the sour cream of wit.'

A candidate for a North Carolina constituency called Frank Grist was furious when the local paper wrote an article which concluded: 'Frank Grist is not qualified to be a dog-catcher.' On the advice of his lawyer he sent a telegram to the newspaper threatening to sue for libel unless it retracted its comments. The paper duly obliged and in the next edition carried the following: 'Frank Grist is fit to be a dog-catcher, but instead of running for that office, he is seeking the post of United States Senator.'

Former Republican Senator and presidential candidate Bob Dole was a formidable politician. I have met him on a number of occasions and have always found him both impressive and witty. However, he has, at times, a vicious tongue which spares no one. Not even himself. This has led to him earning the nickname 'Hatchet Man'.

When Dole was the running-mate of President Gerald Ford in 1976, he unintentionally damaged his own chances during a debate with his opponent Walter Mondale, when he snapped: 'If we added up all those killed and wounded in Democratic wars in this century, it would be about 1.6 million Americans – enough to fill the City of Detroit.' The description of several world conflicts as *Democratic* wars didn't hurt Mondale, it hurt Dole and he knew it. He later quipped: 'I was supposed to go for the jugular and I did – my own.'

In 1972, he was Chairman of the Republican National Committee when the Watergate scandal broke. Asked what he knew about it he quipped: 'I don't know, I was pulling a job in Chicago that night.' He later went on to add: 'Well, we got the burglar vote.' Shortly after this he was dismissed by President Nixon and the role of Chairman was given to George Bush.

Facing Senate re-election in 1974, Dole was worried that the fall-out from Watergate might affect his chance of re-election. His Democratic opponent was Dr Bill Roy, a Roman Catholic who not only supported abortion but who, as a doctor of medicine, had performed a number of abortions as well. During the campaign, when Dole spoke at Roman Catholic Schools, he would say to the children: 'When you go home, ask your mother if she knows how many abortions Dr Roy has performed.' Dole won the election.

Commenting on Congress, Dole said: 'The first month I was there, I wondered how I ever got in. And ever since I've been wondering how the rest of them got in.'

When Dole ran for his party's presidential nomination against George Bush, some party members were concerned that his virulent attacks on Bush would damage the chances of both men. Answering this criticism Dole snapped: 'I will stop telling the truth about Bush, if he stops telling lies about me.'

After a meeting between three ex-presidents Dole commented: 'At a party a few weeks ago, I saw Carter, Ford and Nixon – See No Evil, Hear No Evil and Evil.'

When it was revealed that Richard Nixon had taped all of his White House conversations, Dole quipped: 'Thank goodness whenever I was in the Oval Office I only nodded.'

When President Carter blocked grain sales to the Soviet Union after it had invaded Afghanistan, Dole barked: 'Carter took a poke at the Soviet bear and knocked out the American farmer.'

On fellow Republican, President George Bush: 'He's never had to do a day's work in his life.'

And, again on Bush: 'He never leaves any footprints wherever he goes.'

During the Gulf War, he slammed the Democrats: 'The

Republican strategy is to get Saddam Hussein out of Kuwait. Some of the Democrats' strategy appears to be to get Bush out of the White House.'

On the Clinton administration's changes of direction: 'Clinton's policies need to be checked hourly.'

Commenting on one of his own rather lacklustre and subdued performances: 'I was heavily sedated. It was my night to be nice to everybody.'

On the diminutive Senator John Tower: 'I got a standing ovation from him once and I didn't know the difference.'

And, he made a similar sizist remark about Senator Howard Baker, who was one of his rivals for the 1980 Republican presidential nomination. When Baker dropped out of the race, Dole said: 'He can always open up a tall men's clothing store – in Japan.'

On President Jimmy Carter: 'Southern-fried McGovern.'*

Dole later said: 'I take back calling Jimmy Carter 'Chicken-fried McGovern . . . because I've come to respect McGovern.'

And, on Carter's administration: 'We've had the New Deal, the Fair Deal and now Carter wants to give us a fast deal . . . that will surely end in an ordeal.'

On Democratic Senator Edward Kennedy: 'A phoney. A limousine liberal, a big spender raised on a silver spoon.'

And, on another occasion, he said of Ted Kennedy, in a typical outburst: 'He needs a bridge over troubled waters.'

On Democratic Attorney-General Ramsey Clark: 'A left-leaning marshmallow.'

And, on what to do about fat-cat business supporters: 'Take their money and screw 'em.'

* A reference to the extremely left-wing Democrat George McGovern.

On President Clinton's plan to balance the American budget in ten years, Dole ridiculed: 'There are two ways to get to the top of an oak tree. One is to climb. The other is to find an acorn and sit on it.'

Of course, over the years Dole has made enemies, some of them in his own party. A fellow Republican who was asked to define Dole's views said: 'Oh, that's easy. Bob just waits to see which way the wind is blowing.'

Dole himself once appeared to agree with this verdict, commenting: 'If you're looking for ideology there's Ronald Reagan.'

And, Dole on politics: 'You've got to make hard choices if you're going to be a leader. But if you just want to be a politician you vote no against all the hard things and you vote yes for all the easy things and then you go out and make speeches about how tough you are.'

Amongst his best quips are the following:

'The life jacket of one generation can become the straitjacket of the next.'

'Shame is a powerful weapon.'

President Bill Clinton has been the butt of numerous insults since he came to office. Because he has been perpetually dogged by allegations of impropriety – sexual and financial – it is perhaps not surprising that he has been dubbed in the USA 'The Prince of Sleaze' and 'Slick Willie'.

Although the Paula Jones sexual harassment case against Clinton was thrown out by the US courts in April 1998, no sooner had this occurred than the Monica Lewinsky scandal took off. Although the President was lucky to hang on to office, serious damage has been done to Bill Clinton's reputation. On the political dinner circuit a regular and popular quip is: 'Gallup pollsters interviewed 100 women and asked them if they would sleep with Bill Clinton if it would enhance their career – and 98 replied "Never again".'

In summer 1998, after allegations were first made that Clinton had had an affair with the White House aide Monica Lewinsky, some said that the affair, if proved, could turn out to be 'Clinton's Watergate'. This led one Republican to dub the incident 'Zippergate'. When the press later revealed that Miss Lewinsky was only twenty-one years of age, another referred to the incident as 'Jailbaitgate', adding: 'In this case the smoking gun is in President Clinton's trousers.'

The Lewinsky story broke in America during the 'Unabomber' terrorist trial, leading one wag to call Clinton's scandal 'Unibanger'.

Canadian PM Jean Chrétien said of President Clinton: 'He is not a statesman. He just acts for short-term gain.'

During the last presidential election, the third candidate, the independent Ross Perot, said: 'Nobody likes to be called a liar, but to be called a liar by Bill Clinton is really a unique experience.'

A fellow politician's view of Clinton's foreign policy expertise was provided by Republican Pat Buchanan: 'Bill Clinton's foreign policy experience stems mainly from having breakfasts at the International House of Pancakes.'

Some republicans tell the story that Clinton, despairing of his domestic troubles over sexual impropriety, recently went for a midnight jog around Washington to think and seek inspiration for what he should do.

He stopped at the statue of George Washington, looked up and heard a voice say: 'You must be honest like me – I never told a lie.'

Clinton thought, 'Well, it's too late for me to do that now!' So he continued jogging and reached the statue of Thomas Jefferson. He looked up and heard a voice say, 'Abide by the rules of the Constitution – I should know, I wrote it – and you will inspire the American people.'

'Well,' he thought, 'it's too late for me to do *that* now!' So he turned back to the White House and made a final stop at the statue of the great Republican President Abraham Lincoln. He looked up and said: 'You were a truly great President, even though you were a Republican. Tell me, do you have any suggestions about what I should do?' And he heard a voice say: 'Have you ever thought of going to the theatre?'

Overheard at a Democratic Party meeting: 'I think Clinton's got vision, determination, and tremendous leadership qualities. It's such a pity she's married to that slob Bill.'

During a particularly volatile day on the stock market, a Congressman was overheard to say: 'The Dow Jones has been up and down more often than Clinton's pants.'

And, overheard in Washington, on why Hillary Clinton has stayed loyal to husband Bill: 'Hillary only weighs 95 pounds. The rest is thick skin.'

Dismissing Clinton's claims that allegations against him were just part of a right-wing conspiracy, one Republican said: 'He's just Arkan-sore.'

Republican Congressman commenting on Bill Clinton, after the impeachment process had begun: 'Not so much a lame duck as a dead duck.'

And: 'He ought to be addressed as President Cling-on.'

And, a Tory MP on Clinton: 'His head is like a door-knob – any girl can turn it.'

When one Democrat recently said that America's political

system was like a 'huge melting pot' a Republican silenced him with the riposte: 'Yes, and that's why all the scum rises to the top.'

One recent quip going round Westminster is that President Clinton initially denied that the results of the DNA test on Monica Lewinksy's dress were reliable, and claimed that the marks were no more than 'soup stains'. Hearing this, Kenneth Starr, the prosecutor exclaimed: 'Well, if that's a soup stain, it's gotta be Cockie-Leekie.'

In Washington, the latest Clinton jibe doing the rounds is the story of an occasion when Bill and Hillary are attending a State fair. After the proceedings, the first couple are walking around the site when a trucker hoots his horn as he passes and shouts out of his window: 'Hi Hillary.'
'Who was that?' enquires the President.
'Oh, that's Dean. I used to date him at high school.' Hillary answers.
The President smiles smugly: 'Well dear, just think. If you'd have married him, you'd now be married to a long-distance trucker.'
Hillary is unmoved: 'No Bill. If I had married him, *he* would now be President of the United States.'

Two politicians were talking recently in the wake of the Clinton sex-scandal, one an American Democrat and the other a British Conservative MP. The Democrat, clearly embarrassed, tried to change the subject and started criticizing Britain's regal pomp and ceremony at State functions. He argued that the American system led to more efficient government as President Clinton did not have to take part in obsolete ostentatious routines when he was on official duties. The British Tory appeared unmoved and unimpressed with this argument. 'Oh, in Britain it's not as bad as you make out,' he began. 'In *our* country young students meeting our Head of State are only expected to drop down on one knee.'

And, in a similar vein, when one Senator was asked what the difference was between Bill Clinton and the British actor Hugh Grant, he received the riposte: 'One is a second-rate actor whose career nosedived after it was revealed a young woman gave him oral sex – and the other is the star of the film *Four Weddings and a Funeral.*'

On the 1992 presidential election when voters were faced with a choice of either George Bush, Bill Clinton or Ross Perot, one politician commented: 'Choosing between those three was like needing clean underwear but being forced to decide between three dirty pairs.'

Anonymous on Vice-President Al Gore: 'He is in danger of becoming all things to no people.'

California Governor Republican Pete Wilson on his Democratic opponents: 'They can kiss my rear end – if they can leap that high.'

A story is told in the lower house of a Congressman and his wife who were fast asleep in bed when a noise from downstairs woke her. Waking the Congressman from his slumbers, she said: 'Darling, I think there's a thief in the house.' Ignoring her and turning over he said: 'Maybe in the Senate, my dear, but certainly not in the House.'

Anonymous on one particular Senator: 'They just called him the town drunk. However, he lived in New York at the time.'

Overheard on Capitol Hill: 'In South Africa, most politicians seem to spend a lot of time in jail before they are elected. Here in the USA it's the other way round.'

On one heavy-drinking Congressman: 'He drinks so much, he's been officially declared a beverage.'

ANONYMOUS
MALICE

Over the years many insults thrown outside the chamber have been remembered – as have some of the targets – but not always the perpetrators. Here are some of the best.

*

'She has a face that would fade flowers.' Tory MP on Glenda Jackson.

*

On the late Sir Angus Maude: 'He had so many cavities he spoke with an echo.'

*

On former Tory PM Sir Alec Douglas-Home: 'I have seen better-looking faces on pirate flags.'

*

'The motto of New Labour's government Whips' office is: "If you are nice – you lose." '

*

'He is a very lucky MP – his secretary's lipstick is the same colour as his wife's.'

*

On a particular New Labour MP: 'She has been in more beds than a packet of seeds.'

*

On David Davis MP, currently Chairman of the all-powerful Public Accounts Committee: 'He's the kind of person who would throw a drowning man both ends of the rope.'

*

On former MP Andrew Mitchell: 'He was always willing to lend a helping hand to the one above him.'

'Did you know that when John Prescott was only three months old he was left on a doorstep for three days and three nights in a little basket and nobody picked him up . . . so his mother and father took him in again.'

*

On Paddy Ashdown: 'There are two sides to every question – and he always takes both.'

*

A Tory MP who nearly lost his seat said recently: 'Towards the end of his term as Prime Minister, John Major said to me: "Things just can't go on like this for the Conservative Party." He was right of course. A year later, they got worse!'

*

On Tony Blair: 'He is extremely brave, fearlessly exchanging a quip or two with vicious interviewers like Des O'Connor.'

*

On Tory Marion Roe MP: 'She has her hair done at Interflora.'

*

Labour MP on former minister Nigel Griffiths: 'Nigel? I love every bone in his head.'

*

On Tory David Liddington MP: 'When he speaks he doesn't know what to do with his hands. It's a pity he doesn't put them over his mouth.'

*

'A statesman is a politician who didn't get caught.'

*

Anonymous on a gay New Labour minister: 'He's very decisive. He leaves out all the bull and just takes himself by the horn.'

*

'The House of Commons is a rather odd place – an MP gets up to speak – and says nothing. Nobody listens – and then everybody disagrees.'

*

'He has a black belt in karate – he's not that good, he just doesn't wash it.'

*

On Tony Blair: 'He's the Karaoke Kid – he'd sing anything to get re-elected.'

*

On Labour back-bencher Lawrence Cunliffe MP: 'He has nothing to say but you have to listen a long time to find that out.'

*

On John Prescott: 'He's got a terrible inferiority complex – and he's right.'

*

On Heritage Secretary Chris Smith: 'The difference between Chris Smith and yoghurt is that yoghurt has real culture.'

*

On Chairman of the 1922 Committee, Tory Sir Archie Hamilton MP: 'He's so tall, he has to have his passport photo taken by satellite.'

*

'Hapless Harriet' – Tory MP on former Labour Cabinet Minister Harriet Harman MP.

*

On Tory MP Ann Widdecombe: 'She would make a great distant relative.'

*

And again on Miss Widdecombe: 'Doris Karloff.'

*

In September 1997, after the tragic death of Princess Diana, one Labour MP suggested that London's Heathrow Airport should be renamed in Diana's memory. This caused one former Tory whip to explode: 'I don't think that's a good idea. Who would want to fly to Bird-brain Airport?'

*

On John Prescott: 'Whenever he gets an idea in his head it's a stowaway.'

*

'Lord (Jeffrey) Archer says he will be Lord Mayor of London one day – and I think one day will be quite long enough.'

*

Of a Labour councillor who was invariably inebriated: 'He joined Alcoholics Anonymous. He still drinks but under an assumed name.'

*

On Tory MP Nicholas Soames: 'He can trace his ancestors back to royalty - King Kong.'

*

On the late Jo Richardson MP: 'She was such a bad driver her driving licence had a picture of St Christopher in it and her car was insured with Lloyds of Oops.'

*

On Labour's Maria Fyfe MP: 'She doesn't hold a conversation - she strangles it.'

*

An MP's definition of the First Rule of Journalism: 'All journalists follow this simple rule: "First simplify, then exaggerate." '

*

Overheard on Junior Minister Stephen Timms: 'He looks just like a comic character from the Bash Street Kids.'

*

Labour MP on Peter Mandelson: 'Peter can come and live next door to me anytime - my house is next to a cemetery.'

*

A Tory on defeated Cabinet minister Michael Portillo: 'He has child-bearing lips.'

*

On former MP Sir John Stokes: 'He has more crust than a pie factory.'

*

A Labour MP's view of Jack Straw: 'He is about as much use as a ribless umbrella.'

*

'His open mind should be closed for repairs.' Back-bench MP on Paddy Ashdown. Bolsover MP Dennis Skinner was more direct. After revelations about Mr Ashdown having an affair, Mr Skinner insisted on calling him 'Paddy Pantsdown'.

*

'My wife is so frigid, when she opens her mouth a light goes on.'

*

On one former Tory MP who during his last parliament ran into financial problems, a colleague said: 'He has a black belt in borrowing.'

*

On Archie Hamilton MP: 'He's so tall his shadow has a hinge.'

*

Whips' office motto: 'In politics, a back-bencher must learn to rise above principle.'

*

On one particular female Labour MP, who is a single mother: 'She named her baby after the father – Army!'

*

And, on the same MP: 'She's been boarded more times than the Orient Express.'

*

Sometimes the insulting banter takes on a life of its own. Commenting on former Tory minister Steve Norris, who might be a candidate for London's first Lord Mayor, and who, according to the press, once had five mistresses, one Tory colleague recently said: 'A case of too much Dick and not enough Whittington.'

*

This caused another politician to allude to Mr Norris's former position as a junior transport minister and riposte: 'Well you can't blame him really. Sex is rather like the problems he encountered with transport. Like a bus, you wait a long while and then five come along at once.' Another colleague accepted this explanation: 'Well, I suppose there is always room for another one on top.'

*

'John Prescott is doing the best he can. There, that's scared you.'

*

'The only curve on her body is her Adam's apple.'

*

On Peter Mandelson: 'He doesn't have his hair cut, he goes for an oil change.'

*

On Eddie Loyden MP: 'You know that organization that freezes bodies – well he is a founder member.'

*

'Most journalists I know work eight hours a day and sleep eight hours a day. The trouble is they're the same eight hours.'

*

On Glenda Jackson MP: 'She has the body of a twenty-year-old. . . . a twenty-year-old Skoda.'

*

On David Winnick MP: 'I don't know how old he is but when he was young the Dead Sea was still alive.'

*

On Ian McCartney MP: 'He's so short, when he sits he's taller.'

*

And again on Mr McCartney: 'When it rains he's the last to know.'

*

On former Tory Whip, David Davis MP: 'If he worked on a suicide-prevention hot line, he would take the phone off the hook.'

*

On Andrew Mackay MP: 'To him a game of golf isn't a matter of life and death – it's more important than that.'

*

On Michael Heseltine MP: 'He's so rich, he has bookcases just for his bankbooks.'

*

On the Members' Cafeteria: 'It's the only place where you say grace over grease.'

*

'He is so thick he thinks that "Vat 69" is the Pope's phone number.'

*

According to one Labour MP, the definition of 'confusion' is Fathers' Day at a Tribune Meeting.

*

'I bet she closes her eyes when her husband makes love – she doesn't want to see him having a good time.'

*

On former Labour Cabinet minister Barbara, now Baroness, Castle: 'She is so old that on her birthday her family open a magnum of Wincarnis.'

*

At the Labour end of the Commons Tea Room the story is told of two MPs on an overseas trip to Canada, one of them Labour, the other a Tory. Trekking through the woods they get lost and suddenly find themselves confronted by a 500-pound grizzly bear. The Labour MP stoops down, pulls a pair of running shoes out of his rucksack and puts them on. Noticing this, the Tory MP starts laughing. 'Goodness me, you Labour chaps don't know anything about wildlife or the countryside, do you? You stupid duffer. You'll never outrun a grizzly bear, old boy.' Turning on his heels, the Labour MP shouts back: 'I don't have to outrun the grizzly – I just have to outrun you!'

*

On Tony Blair: 'He's just embarked on a boast-to-boast tour.'

*

On Ann Widdecombe MP: 'She's "pushing thirty-five" so long it's pleated.'

*

Again, on Ann Widdecombe: 'The way she finds fault, you'd think there was a reward.'

*

'Edward Heath doesn't have an enemy in the world. . . . he's outlived them.'

*

'Silence is a long conversation with Lord Ryder.'

*

'He has the manners of a gentleman – I knew they couldn't belong to him.'

*

Young Tory on a female Labour MP: 'She has the looks that turn heads. Tory Whip: ' . . . and stomachs too.'

*

On Tony Banks MP: 'He thinks "pause" is a disease.'

*

'In her house the antique furniture is just stuff from her first marriage.'

*

On Dennis Turner MP: 'He has a great voice . . . unfortunately it's in someone else's throat.'

*

'He's so unlucky he probably gets paper cuts from get-well cards.'

*

On John Prescott MP: 'He should leave and let live.'

*

Overheard on former MP Andrew Faulds: 'His way of being right is to be wrong at the top of his voice.'

*

'He is so thin, the crease in his trousers is him.'

*

'She is so ugly, her make-up comes in a snake-bite kit.'

*

On Frank Dobson: 'He has a walk-in mouth.'

*

On Tessa Jowell MP: 'She has a new form of exercise – aerobic nagging.'

*

On Peter Mandelson: 'Whenever he enters a room, he gets a cringing ovation.'

*

On former MP and Leader of the House Tony (now Lord) Newton: 'He smokes four packs of cigarettes a day because it gives his hands something to do - shake!'

*

'She has a lot of class - steerage.'

*

On one new female Labour MP: 'When she has one drink, she can't feel it. When she has two drinks, she can feel it. After her third drink, anybody can feel it.'

*

On Labour's Tony Banks: 'He speaks at 120 words a minute - with gusts up to 150.'

*

On Tory Ian Bruce MP: 'He's suffering from a non-entity crisis.'

*

On Archie Norman MP: 'I won't say he's conceited but if you asked him to name the Seven Wonders of the World, he would probably mention himself twice!'

*

On one particular female MP: 'Some women have faces that can stop a clock. She could stop Switzerland!'

*

On the late Sir Nicholas Fairbairn: 'A chain drinker.'

*

And again on Sir Nicholas: 'He never drinks unless he's alone or with someone.'

*

A Labour back-bencher was overheard to remark recently: 'In our New Labour Government, ministers are not just bound by collective responsibility, they're bound and gagged!'

*

On former MP Edwina Currie: 'Knowing her, I bet she'll even deny that she's getting wrinkles and will claim her skin's turning to corduroy.'

*

'I heard John Prescott's speech under very unfortunate circumstances – my seat faced the platform.'

*

On Charles Kennedy MP: 'He would make a perfect stranger.'

*

On Robin Cook: 'He's really moving but that's because he's going downhill.'

*

On a Whip: 'He has knifed more people than a surgeon.'

*

On one particular MP: 'He was descended from a long line his mother fell for.'

*

On Ken Livingstone: 'He was an unwanted child. When they gave him a rattle it was still attached to the snake.'

*

On David Davis MP: 'He always sees germs in the milk of human kindness.'

*

'He's a born-again cretin.'

*

Tory Whip commenting on former minister Phillip Openheimer: 'He has a good head on his shoulders – a different one each night.'

*

'He drinks so much, when he sweats he's a fire hazard.'

*

On Tony Blair: 'These days he is so conceited, he calls "Dial-a-Prayer" and asks for his messages.'

*

On William Hague MP: 'He sounds like a cross between Harold Wilson and Wilfred Pickles.'

*

On Peter Mandelson: He's always me-deep in conversation.'

*

On John Prescott: 'The closest he'll come to a brainstorm is a slow drizzle.'

*

On Charles Kennedy: 'He's nobody's fool. He freelances.'

*

'The only thing she ever gives is in.'

*

Labour MP: 'In my constituency, if you pay the rent on time, they arrest you for robbery.'

*

On former MP Alan Glyn: 'He was born in the Year of Our Lord only knows.'

*

On one new labour woman MP, known for flirting: 'She used to live in all the best hotels . . . one hour at a time.'

*

'I think William Hague is just like Winston Churchill. Both look like new-born babies.'

*

On Gwyneth Dunwoody MP: 'She has an unlisted dress size.'

*

'What has five heads, ten legs and three teeth?' Answer: the front row at a Fabian meeting.

*

Overheard in the Members' Tea Room:
First MP: 'I hear you have a water bed.'
Second MP: 'With *my* wife in it, it's the Dead Sea.'

*

On Barbara Follett MP: 'She's so rich, the bags under her eyes are Gucci.'

*

And again on Mrs Follett: 'The only person I know who puts Perrier in her steam iron.'

*

On former MP Charles Goodson-Wickes: 'Proof that no shirt is too young to be stuffed.'

*

On the late Tory MP Sir David Lightbown, a former Tory Whip: 'He never hits a man when he's down. He kicks him.'

*

'Some people say she's a pain in the back. Others have a lower opinion of her.'

*

On John Major: 'For years he was an unknown failure. Now he is a known failure.'

*

On Chris Smith MP (who admits that he is gay): 'He believes in vice versa.'

*

On former Tory Deputy Leader Peter Lilley: 'He looks like a cross between Dr Niles Crane from the TV show *Frasier* and Ted Lune.'

*

On a former minister: 'She talks so much she's listed in the Guinness Book of Broken Records.'

*

First MP: 'I've heard that William Hague hasn't got life insurance.'
Second MP: 'Why?'
First MP: 'Nobody knows his policy.'

*

On Peter Mandelson: 'He's got a good sense of rumour.'

*

On former MP Tim Sainsbury: 'He's so rich, when he catches a plane he has to check in his wallet.'

*

And again on Mr Sainsbury: 'He made his money the old-fashioned way. He inherited it.'

*

'At least the Commons Dining-Room is consistent – they serve steak, coffee and ice cream – all at the same temperature.'

*

On Peter Mandelson: 'He's got about as many friends as an alarm clock.'

*

On Tony Blair: 'He claims to speak to the Lord – on a one-to-one basis.'

*

On Gary Streeter MP: 'He's so religious, when he was a minister all his papers were marked "Top Sacred".'

*

'I'm all in favour of women MPs. It's better having them in the House than outside driving cars.'

*

On former Tory MP Michael Bates: 'He's so religious he wears stained-glass contact lenses.'

*

On Labour's Kevin Barron: 'He puts the rust into rustic.'

*

When one Conservative asked his wife what suit he should wear to attend a speech by Archie Norman, he received the reply: 'Your track suit.'

*

'Put two Northern Ireland MPs on a desert island and within a week there would be three churches.'

*

Alluding to the practice of voter impersonation, one MP claimed to have heard an election report from Ireland which stated: 'With three cemeteries still to be heard from, the election is too close to call.'

*

'She has a 38-inch bust – and an IQ to match.'

*

'He has every attribute of a dog except loyalty.'

*

Overheard in Strangers Bar: 'I hit John Prescott yesterday. I will probably be charged with "Fair Play".'

*

On civil servants: 'To err is human, to shrug is civil service.'

*

Sometimes a blow arrives from an unexpected quarter. One December, a politician was informed by his secretary that the political editor of the *Star*, his regional paper, had telephoned and wanted to know what the MP wanted for Christmas.

Flattered, the MP told her to phone him back. 'Tell them nothing really,' he said 'But if they insist, tell them a large bottle of whisky and a box of mints would be nice.'
On Christmas eve the paper carried a seasonal story on its centre pages: 'Prime Minister Tony Blair wants world peace this Christmas; William Hague wants the richer Western nations to help prevent war and famine in the poorer Third World countries AND your local MP says he wants "a large bottle of whisky and a box of mints".'

*

Despite the take-over of Skoda cars by VW, the gibes at the marque have continued. The following were overheard in the Commons:

*

What do you call a Skoda at the top of a hill? A bloody miracle.

And: What's the difference between a Skoda and a dress worn by Kate Moss?
You get a tit in a Skoda.

*

In the Commons Tea Room the story was told of how, when leaving the Commons one night, William Hague fell into the Thames and got into difficulty. Hearing his cries for help as he left, the Prime Minister dived in and fished him out. Rather embarrassed, Hague thanked Blair for his rescue but said

nervously, 'Please don't leak it to the press that I can't swim.'
Blair looked at him equally nervously: 'All right,' he agreed,
'provided also that you don't leak it to the press that I can't
walk on water.'

*

Further Commons Tea Room comment: 'The IRA leaders
have told their men to equip themselves for germ warfare –
so their supporters have all bought themselves septic tanks.'

*

Although it is no longer fashionable to talk ill of our European
partners, during the Second World War things were different.
Then the gossip at Westminster was whether you had 'heard
the one about the Italian soldier who deserted his regiment
and stood his ground'. But the most popular quip at the time
was about the Italian soldier who 'drew his sword. . . . and
cut up a side street'. One wag even described the Italian flag
as 'a white cross on a white background'.

*

In these Europhile times, surprisingly things are not all that
different. One MP was recently explaining that when Euro-
peans die they all go to heaven or hell: 'The difference is
that in heaven the English are the police, the French the
cooks, the Germans the mechanics, the Italians the lovers
and the Swiss organize everything. Whereas, in hell, the
Germans are the police, the English the cooks, the French
the mechanics, the Swiss the lovers and the Italians organize
everything.'

*

In the 1980s, after the Falklands War, the question was: 'Why
does the new Argentinian navy have glass-bottom boats?'
'To see the *old* Argentinian navy.'

*

Upon seeing an Iranian and a Spanish politician talking, a
Whip remarked: 'There's Oil of Olé.'

*

William Hague is so young that many pensioners have food in their fridge that is older.

*

Anonymous on Prince Charles: 'He claims that he's environmentally friendly but he doesn't want to upset business, so he talks to plants. The plant at Sellafield, the plant at Douneray and the plant at three mile island.'

*

Anonymous on Lord (Roy) Jenkins: 'The only thing he ever fought for was a table for two at the Mirabelle.'

*

On Archie Norman MP: 'I won't say he's big-headed but his hats are made in a tent factory.'

*

On Tony Blair's style of government: 'This is a government run by spin-obsessed ministers living in trendy Notting Hill. It has everything to do with wooing middle England and staying in power and absolutely nothing to do with representing the working classes.'

*

A Tory on former Tory MP Edwina Currie: 'At Christmas I'd like to hang her and kiss the mistletoe.'

*

On Tony Blair's Press Office: 'They work so hard, the only regular exercise they get is stretching the truth.'

*

On Tory Ann Widdecombe MP: 'She has a tongue that could clip a hedge.'

*

'You have a wonderful head on your shoulders. Whose is it?'

*

'Why don't you freeze your teeth and give your tongue a sleigh ride?'

*

'You're a great argument for the death penalty.'

*

'The stork that brought you should have been fined for smuggling dope.'

*

'I see it's not only the wall that's plastered.'

*

'I can see with you ignorance is a religion.'

*

'The gentleman is obviously well past his yell-by date.'

*

'Is that your face, or are you wearing a ski-mask?'

*

'Why don't you put an egg in your shoe and beat it?'

*

'Some people bring happiness wherever they go. He brings happiness whenever he goes.'

*

And, a final word on politicians: 'If you ever see a politician who pleases everybody, he will be neither sitting on the left, nor standing on the right. He will be lying flat and there will be a lot of flowers around him.'

PUT-DOWNS

With the advent of television and most political parties now using video mail-shots, the public meeting is not what it was. Indeed, in most constituencies it now does not exist at all. This is a great pity. On TV and video all we see from our politicians are pre-scripted, and sometimes somewhat bland performances. Today, even when a party leader attends a 'live' rally, because the television cameras are present the party managers ensure that the audience is exclusively composed of invited supporters, thus the likelihood of the politician putting down a heckler is negligible.

It was not always thus. In days gone by, at the political public meeting anything could happen, and sometimes did. Here are some of my favourite put-downs used against hecklers and political opponents by politicians of all parties over the years.

'Brains aren't everything. In your case, they're nothing.'

*

'Sir, you have the face of a saint – a Saint Bernard.'

*

'Don't you ever get tired of having yourself around?'

*

'Don't worry. There is a good reason for you to have that stupid look on your face. You are stupid.'

*

'Well, I'd like to leave a thought with you – but where would you put it?'

*

'I know you weren't born yesterday – nobody could get that ugly in twenty-four hours.'

*

'You know, you are so dull, you can't even entertain a doubt.'

*

'I have nothing but confidence in you – and not a lot of that.'

*

'Sir, it's a good thing for you that mirrors can't laugh.'

*

'You obviously have a lot of time on your hands and the wrinkles to prove it.'

*

'She's not pushing forty – she's dragging it.'

*

'He has no equals – only superiors.'

*

'I am sure you also use your head – mostly for a rock garden.'

*

When a heckler shouted: 'I was born Labour, I have lived as a Labour man and I'm going to die Labour,' the Tory candidate said: 'So much for your ambition.'

*

'You're obviously not yourself today. Enjoy it while you can.'

*

'I'm told men drink to your face – they'd have to.'

*

'If I had a lower IQ, I'm sure I'd enjoy your company.'

*

A heckler shouted at an MP: who had just told an old joke: 'That joke was your father's.' The MP shot back: 'And you were your mother's.'

*

'I know you are a legend in your own mouth.'

*

'Why don't you go home now? Your cage has been cleaned.'

*

'You should have your ears cleaned out . . . with a 12-bore shotgun.'

*

'I am sure you're kind to your inferiors . . . but where do you find them?'

*

'You're as useful as a one-legged man trying to put out a grass fire.'

*

'If you were alive you'd be a very sick man.'

*

'I'd make you eat those words if you had teeth.'

*

'You've got the sort of face I'd like to shake hands with.'

*

'Someone get a plumber – there's a big drip in here.'

*

'I can see you started at the bottom . . . and sank.'

*

'I wish my future was as bright as your suit. There's enough grease on your clothes to fry a pan of chips.'

*

'Your mouth is big enough to sing duets.'

*

'I've seen better arguments in a bowl of alphabet soup.'

*

'I may not agree with what you say but I'll defend to the death your right to shut up.'

*

'Go and see a mind-reader. You'll get in for half-price.'

*

'You're the sort who gives idiots a bad name.'

*

'Did I see you at the Nuremberg trials?'

*

'If they put a price on your head – take it.'

*

'You have a wonderful head on your shoulders. Whose is it?'

*

'Why don't you freeze your teeth and give your tongue a sleigh ride?'

*

'You're a great argument for the death penalty.'

*

'The stork that brought you should have been fined for smuggling dope.'

*

'I see it's not only the wall that's plastered.'

*

'I can see with you ignorance is a religion.'

*

'The gentleman is obviously well past his yell-by date.'

*

And, a final word on politicians: 'If you ever see a politician who pleases everybody, he will be neither sitting on the left, nor standing on the right. He will be lying flat and there will be a lot of flowers around him.'

INDEX